The Gospel According to Leviticus

THE GOSPEL ACCORDING TO LEVITICUS

The Gospel According to Leviticus

978-1-952542-05-3
978-1-952542-06-0 eBook

DAVID KALAS

The Gospel According to
Leviticus
Finding God's Love
in God's Law

3x5 Press
www.The3x5Club.com

THE GOSPEL ACCORDING TO LEVITICUS:
Finding God's Love in God's Law

978-1-952542-05-3

To my Mother,
whose constant love when I was a child
still helps me to understand God's love as an adult.

Contents

Introduction
Rave Reviews

When I go online to shop for something, if I feel any uncertainty about the purchase I am making, I will take a few minutes to read the reviews. This is one of the fascinating features of the new world in which consumers live and shop. Attached to the very description of the product you want to buy, you can find a whole host of ratings and reviews from people who have already bought and used it.

I know there have been purchases I have decided against because of some unfavorable reviews. And, likewise, glowing reviews have often helped me make my choice. Perhaps you've had similar experiences.

With that in mind, then, let me share with you a few reviews that come from the pages of Scripture. They are all reviews of the same product. Consider, as you read them, whether you would make that purchase.

"_____ *is my delight.*"

"My soul is consumed with longing for _____
at all times."

*"*_____ *makes me wiser than all those*
around me."

*"*_____ *is perfect, it revives my soul."*

"Happy are those who have _____."

"I delight in _____ *because I love it."*

"At midnight I rise to give thanks to God for
_____."

*"*_____ *is sweeter than honey and more*
desirable than gold."

"Seven times a day I praise _____."

*"*_____ *is everlasting."*

You read reviews like that, and you say to yourself, "I've gotta have that!" So you click on the button to add it to your cart. You place the order enthusiastically, and you're filled with excitement when, two days later, the box is delivered to your house.

You open the box like a child at Christmas. You pull out the packing material. You look inside. And you find . . . the Book of Leviticus.

Offerings. Holy days. Dietary codes. Ritual cleanliness. Sexual boundaries. How to respond to certain spreading diseases in skin, on clothing, and in houses.

You begin shuffling through the packing material inside the box. "Is there supposed to be something else in here?" "Did they send me the wrong thing?" "Could it be that this—this!—is what earned such high praise from other users?"

You do find other things in the box besides Leviticus, but it's not necessarily that much more promising. There are the instructions and dimensions for the Tabernacle from the Book of Exodus. There's some case law about offerings, a few details about priests and Levites, and instructions about a red heifer from the Book of Numbers. And there's also the Book of Deuteronomy.

The "product" that earns such rave reviews in Scripture, you see, is God's Law. It is said to be true, perfect, and eternal. It is celebrated as a source of wisdom, guidance, and delight. It inspires in its adherents love, devotion, and righteousness.

The ancient Jews regarded the Law as the articulation of their covenant with God, as the guide for living, and as the bedrock of their Scriptures. Contemporary American Christians, by contrast, tend to regard the Law as tedious and irrelevant. We treat it as optional for reading and optional for living.

Why the great divergence? How can the same "product" earn such dramatically different reviews?

Years ago, while visiting an older member of my congregation in his home, he proudly took me on a tour of his workshop. I do a little tinkering myself, and so I was naturally interested in his tools and equipment, his projects, and organization. Along the way, he showed me his scroll saw—a tool I didn't have in my workshop. In fact, I had never seen one up close before. And so I asked him what it could do, and he grabbed a piece of scrap wood and showed me.

What he created in just a few minutes was remarkable. And so, as you might guess, it wasn't too many days later that I bought a scroll saw for my workshop. Once I had it unwrapped, set up, and had hastily read the directions, I eagerly selected a piece of wood on which to work some magic. And, well, it was a disaster. About the only good thing I can say about my experiment is that I still have all my fingers.

I had asked that gentleman from my congregation what a scroll saw could do. I should have asked, instead, "What can you do with a scroll saw?" For just because a *scroll saw* can do it doesn't mean that *I* can.

The point is that there is a learning curve in almost every area of life. Not much of significance is mastered quickly. From shooting free throws to playing the violin, any skill needs to be developed. And, at another level, our senses need to be developed too. The food connoisseur has a fuller appreciation for a gourmet meal than I do. The trained musician will hear and appreciate things at a concert that I will not. The art student will see and enjoy elements of a painting that are unrecognized by me.

I would be foolish, you see, to debate with that gentleman from my congregation about the limitations of a scroll saw. The limitations were within me. I should, instead, learn from him how to use the tool. And, likewise, I might do well to learn from the connoisseur, the musician, and the artist, rather than dismissing the thing that I don't fully appreciate.

In the same spirit, then, let us humbly withhold our critiques of the Old Testament Law. We read the glowing "reviews" of it, and they prompt us to wonder if there is more there than meets the eye—or at least more than has met our eyes. Perhaps we might yield to the judgment of those who have a better, fuller appreciation for the Law than we do.

The psalmist said God's Law was perfect and that it revives the soul. That is the kind of review that makes me want that product. And if, when I get it home, I don't feel the same enthusiasm or have the same success, then let me learn more about it. That is the goal and purpose of this book.

1
Stopping at Sinai

The LORD our God made a covenant with us at Horeb.
Not with our ancestors did the LORD make this covenant,
but with us, who are all of us here alive today.

Deuteronomy 5:2-3 NRSV

In the beginning . . . there were stories. Quite literally, the first book of the Bible is filled with great stories! The plot moves quickly, the characters are compelling, and the storytelling is skillful. A person who appreciates a good story will find the Book of Genesis easy and enjoyable reading. There are love stories and sibling rivalries. We see complicated marriages, broken relationships, and lovely reunions. We read of kings and battles, blessings and threats, revenge and forgiveness. The story that begins with Creation weaves through the fall and the flood, through covenants, providence, grace, and salvation. The divine hand is prominent and evident at some times, while working marvelously behind-the-scenes at others.

By the time the curtain closes on Genesis, the plot of the story has moved us down to Egypt. And when the curtain opens on Exodus, the story picks up and fast-forwards through four centuries very rapidly. The large, extended family of Jacob moves to Egypt as VIP guests, but after a generation, their circumstances change completely when they are involuntarily transformed from guests to slaves. They live through four hundred years of slavery there before the time of their deliverance comes.

The pace of the storytelling slows in Exodus to tell about that deliverance, and it is a truly compelling story. We follow the recurring confrontations between Moses and Egypt's Pharaoh—a relationship so tantalizing that it has inspired a good deal of creative speculation in film treatments of this biblical event. We watch the series of plagues, as God gradually wears down the nation that enslaves God's people. And then we read the account of the climactic night, when the Hebrews eat a symbolic and hurried meal just prior to being set free from their bondage.

Next thing we know, the scene has moved to the shore of the Red Sea, where God prevails in one final battle with the fatally stubborn Pharaoh. Then the Lord leads the people into the wilderness, providing food, water, and guidance each step of the way. And, finally, halfway through the Book of Exodus, the people and the readers arrive at their first real destination. The ultimate destination for the Hebrew slaves, of course, is the Promised Land. That's what God has in store for them at the end of this journey. But it is not a direct flight. They have a layover. There is a planned, deliberate stop at Mount Sinai between Egypt and Canaan.

We read of the people's arrival at Mount Sinai in Exodus 19. We read of their departure from Mount Sinai in Numbers 10. For those keeping score, there are fifty-seven chapters between that arrival and that departure. You see, then, how dramatically the material changes. As does the pace of the narrative—some would even say that it stops altogether. After so many chapters of stories, during which we were moving through time and space, we now find ourselves immersed in many chapters of Law, parked in one spot for what feels like a very long time.

An Earnest Habit

I grew up with my father's Bible reading example before my eyes. He didn't verbally insist that I follow his example; he didn't need to. His influence was so strong, and my admiration for him was so great, that I naturally observed everything he did.

I had observed two prominent elements of my dad's Bible reading. First, he read every day. This was not a thing he did when he felt like it or when he had the time to get around to it. It was a priority. It was first thing every morning. And, second, he read from cover to cover. I had heard the story of how, when he was still just a boy, the importance of reading the whole Bible was impressed on him by a traveling evangelist. And so, in response to that encouragement and challenge, he read through the Bible from start to finish that year, and he had done it countless times since.

With those two elements of his example prominently before my young, admiring eyes, I resolved to do the same. I decided that I would read through the Bible from start to finish, and I would read every day. And so I began, earnestly, with Genesis 1, and I read every day for many days. But then, after a certain number of days, I broke my pattern. I had gotten into Leviticus, and I found that the reading was difficult for me. Frankly, I didn't feel much interest in picking it back up the next day, and so I didn't. In fact, I let quite a few days pass, and then, when I started again, I literally started again. This was admittedly compulsive, but at least it was earnest. Because I had failed to keep the daily pattern, I made myself go all the way back to the beginning and start over with Genesis 1. And so, with new resolve, I began my daily reading pattern again, planning to read the entire Bible, from beginning to end.

After some days, however, the same thing happened again. I got into the material about the Tabernacle and the sacrifices, and I simply lost interest and stopped. And after some more time passed, I once again renewed my resolve to read the Bible through, and once again I went back to Genesis 1 to start over. I don't know how many different times this pattern repeated itself. And I don't recommend such compulsiveness. But I share that story from my adolescence to let you know that it was not exactly love at first sight when I met the Old Testament Law.

In the end, I came away from that period of my relationship with the Bible very familiar with Genesis and Exodus. And I am also very familiar with the struggles so many Christians have with the Old Testament Law. When the reading reaches Mount Sinai, that is where so many of us stop.

Previous Appointment

We noted above that the children of Israel did not catch a direct flight from Egypt to the Promised Land. They had a scheduled stop along the way. It was a deliberate appointment to meet with God at a very specific place.

The meeting was booked long before the slaves had been freed. Indeed, back at the burning bush, when God was first enlisting Moses for the task at hand, this appointment was built into Israel's calendar. The Lord promised Moses, saying, "Certainly I will be with you, and this shall be the sign to you that it is I who have sent you: when you have brought the people out of Egypt, you shall worship God at this mountain" (Exodus 3:12 NASB).

An important grammatical detail is lost in the English translation. Unlike Hebrew, contemporary English does not naturally distinguish between the plural and the singular second person pronouns. Both come out as *you*. The old King James English, however, offered more precision, with its use of *thee* and *thou* as singular pronouns and *ye* as plural. So the scheduled appointment reads this way: "When thou hast brought forth the people out of Egypt, ye shall serve God upon this mountain" (Exodus 3:12 KJV).

God is saying, "I will be with you, Moses. I have sent you, Moses. And I will give you, Moses, a sign. You, Moses, will bring the people out of Egypt. And then you, *the whole group*, shall worship me here on this mountain."

It's a beautiful image of coming full circle. At this moment, Moses is alone on the mountain with God, and he is receiving a seemingly impossible assignment. The children of Israel, meanwhile, are miles away, languishing in the tight grip of Pharaoh. But the Lord promised that, in the foreseeable future, Moses would be back at that mountain with God, but that next time he would not be at all alone. Instead, he will have with him that whole nation of slaves, and they will worship their Deliverer together at the very place of God's call. Beautiful!

Mount Sinai is not their final home, you see, but it is a destination. It is an essential, scheduled stop along the way. And that is where they receive God's Law.

Life with God 101

When my wife, Karen, was pregnant with our first child, we kept close at hand the book *What to Expect When You're Expecting*. We referenced it often as it walked us through what was new and unfamiliar territory to us. And, likewise, once our daughter was born, we turned to other books and resources to help guide us in our new life as parents.

The children of Israel were entering into a new life. For generations they had been slaves; now they were free. They had been living in one land, but soon they would be living in another. They had lived their lives thus far as the property of others, but soon they would have houses and land of their own. They had been governed by whips and chains, but now they would be governed by God and God's Laws. This was going to be a new life, indeed, and they would need a reference, a resource, to guide them in that new life. God's Law would be that resource. God's Law would guide them.

This was to be more than just a new life circumstantially, however. It was also a new life relationally. In a sense, all of their relationships became new once they were free people. And, most significantly, they were entering into a new relationship with God. Specifically, they were entering into a covenant relationship with God.

Covenant is one of the central, recurring themes of Scripture. In the time of Noah, God established a covenant with humankind and all of creation (Genesis 9:8-17). Later, the Lord initiated a covenant with Abram (Genesis 15:17-21). Israel remembered God making a covenant with David (Psalm 89:3-4). The prophet Jeremiah anticipated the day when God would establish a new covenant with people (Jeremiah 31:31-34). At the Last Supper, Jesus identified the cup as the blood of a new covenant (Matthew 26:27-28). And the apostles celebrated and taught about that new covenant that is available through Christ (for example, 2 Corinthians 3:5-6; Galatians 4:24; Hebrews 7:22).

Covenant was not an exclusively religious or spiritual term. Human beings established covenants with one another as well (for example, 1 Samuel 18:3). But it was understood to be a most solemn alliance, a binding agreement, a pledge. And the beauty of this recurring theme in Scripture is that God is the one who initiates covenants again and again with human beings. That is to say, the Lord makes solemn alliances, enters into binding agreements with people.

This is no small matter. An omnipotent, eternal, sovereign God is under no obligation to make alliances with finite and fallen human creatures. It is sufficient for Almighty God to give commands—one-way instructions. But a covenant suggests a two-way relationship; indeed, it implies a partnership. A commandment is really only binding on the one being commanded. A covenant, on the other hand, has the quality of being mutually binding. And God deigns to initiate such covenants.

So it was there, at Sinai, that the people of Israel entered into a covenant relationship with God. There they received from God the Law, and the centerpiece of that Law—what we know as the Ten Commandments—was carved on two tablets like a contract printed in duplicate. And the copies of that contract were kept in a box, which was known as the ark of the covenant or the covenant box. In short, the Law represented the terms of the covenant relationship between God and the people of Israel.

The Law, then, was Israel's guide and reference book for their new life, their new future, and their new relationship with God. Call it *What to Expect When You Belong to a Holy God*. Meanwhile, inasmuch as you and I are welcomed into a relationship with that same God, and inasmuch as we, too, are given a new life and new future by God, we will find beauty, wisdom, meaning, and guidance in the same reference that the Lord gave to Israel back at Sinai.

The Necessary Stop

A generation of moviegoers will remember the 1984 cult favorite, *The Karate Kid*. A teenager named Daniel is tutored in karate by the elderly Mr. Miyagi. The problem is that it doesn't feel at all to Daniel like karate is what he is learning. Instead, so far as he can tell, he is just being required to do chores—mindlessly repetitive chores—like painting a fence and waxing a car. At a critical moment in the training process, however, the method suddenly becomes clear. Mr. Miyagi was training Daniel's hands and arms to do their parts of the action.

Waxing a car is not self-defense. Painting a fence is not winning a match. But the wise instructor knew that those chores were necessary steps toward the ultimate goal. The chores were means to an end. Practicing actions that were not inherently karate proved to be training for karate.

Long before *The Karate Kid* hit the theaters, the Lord God had already employed such training for his people. "The Law has become our tutor," Paul wrote to the Galatians, "to lead us to Christ" (Galatians 3:24). Did the people of Moses' day recognize Christ in the holy days, in the priesthood, or in the Tabernacle? No more than Daniel recognized karate in car waxing, I suspect. But the Law was part of the process.

Both Paul and the writer of Hebrews use the image of a shadow. "The law is only a shadow of the good things that are coming—not the realities themselves" (Hebrews 10:1 NIV). "These are a shadow of the things that were to come, the reality, however, is found in Christ" (Colossians 2:17 NIV). So it is that we refer to foreshadowings of Christ that are contained in the Old Testament, and especially in the Law.

Likewise, the elements of the Old Testament Law point to some greater reality beyond themselves. They are like the old connect-the-dot puzzles we had as children. Before the lines were drawn, the picture was unrecognizable. Once the connections were made, however, then it all became clear. So it is that, in Christ, the dots are connected, the picture is colored in, and we recognize that it was all a portrait of the Son of God. Similarly, the dots of the Old Testament Law all come together to form the same picture.

Luke tells us a story that helps to illustrate the point. On Easter Sunday afternoon, two of Jesus' disciples were traveling to the town of Emmaus. While on the road, Jesus met up with them and conversed with them along the way. As they talked, it became clear that the men were bewildered by the events of recent days. And so, "beginning with Moses and with all the prophets, [Jesus] explained to them the things concerning Himself in all the Scriptures" (Luke 24:27).

The use of Moses' name here is a reference to the Old Testament Law. And so we discover, along with that first generation of disciples, that the things that had happened to Jesus were not random, accidental, or surprising. Rather, all of it was anticipated and even foreshadowed. What Jesus did was the fulfillment of promise and prophecy. He was the reality hinted at by the shadows seen in the Law of Moses.

In this way, then, we see just how necessary a stop Sinai was along the way for Christians. It was not just part of the physical itinerary between Egypt and the Promised Land; it was a part of a theological journey too. It was necessary, not only for that immediate generation of Hebrews (completing their journey) but also for the larger population of God's people across the millennia. The Law is a place we go through on our way to Christ. Indeed, the Law helps us to get to him.

The Road of Discipleship

Sinai continues to be a necessary stop for us today. Let us not think that the usefulness of the Law was exhausted in Moses' generation. Even the fulfillment of the Law in Jesus is not a reason to pack it up and put it away on a shelf. Rather, the Law continues to be an essential part of the journey for those who follow Jesus.

Interestingly, Jesus himself elevates the importance of commandments for his followers. Too often, Christians have used Christ as a sort of hall pass to get them out of the Law. But that is a misunderstanding of his teaching and his role.

Near the beginning of the Sermon on the Mount, Jesus minced no words about the continuing importance of God's Law: "Do not think that I came to abolish the Law or the Prophets; I did not come to abolish but to fulfill. For truly I say to you, until heaven and earth pass away, not the smallest letter or stroke shall pass from the Law until all is accomplished. Whoever then annuls one of the least of these commandments, and teaches others *to do* the same, shall be called least in the kingdom of heaven; but whoever keeps and teaches *them*, he shall be called great in the kingdom of heaven" (Matthew 5:17-19).

Jesus also impressed upon his disciples the relational dynamic of commandments and obedience. We gather from his critique of the Pharisees that they were often guilty of a sort of heartless and mindless legalism. And their example is not meant to be our model. "For I tell you that unless your righteousness surpasses that of the Pharisees and the teachers of the law, you will certainly not enter the kingdom of heaven" (Matthew 5:20 NIV). In contrast to the Pharisees' faulty example, however, we are taught that obeying the Lord's commands is meant to be a matter of love (John 14:15).

And, finally, we discover that obeying the Lord's commands is essential to discipleship. Jesus' final recorded instruction to his disciples in the Gospel of Matthew is known as The Great Commission. He said to them, "Go and make disciples of all nations, baptizing them in the name of the Father and of the Son and of the Holy Spirit, and teaching them to obey everything I have commanded you" (Matthew 28:19-20 NIV).

The recipe for discipleship, you see, is baptism and teaching. Baptism is the entry point. The teaching is what equips and guides us for daily living as disciples. And the content of that teaching is to obey the Lord's commands.

We said that Mount Sinai was an essential, scheduled stop along the way for the Hebrew slaves. That mountain serves as a metaphor for the Law that was given there. And the Law, too, is an essential, scheduled stop along the way for the people of God today. It is not our final home, but it is a necessary part of the journey—the journey to Christ and the journey of following him.

2
It All Begins with a *Who*

I am the LORD *your God, who brought you out of the
land of Egypt to give you the land of Canaan* and *to be
your God.*

Leviticus 25:38

I heard a pastor recently preach a sermon about the Ten
Commandments. It was not what I expected. My assumption—and
my own practice as a preacher—is that one chooses to preach from a
text because of what it has to offer. Evidently, however, this colleague
did not feel that way about the Ten Commandments. On the contrary,
he used the Ten Commandments as a jumping off place for ridiculing
the Old Testament Law as a whole. In fact, along the way he assured
his congregation, "You can basically just throw out anything that's
in the Old Testament." His sermon was full of humor, which made
it very appealing. A spoonful of sugar helps the heresy go down. But
still I was astonished by what I had heard.

His statement was a sloppy one, of course, for I'm sure he doesn't want his people throwing out the Twenty-Third Psalm, the commandments to love God and neighbor, or Micah's good summary of what the Lord requires. It was also a theologically careless remark, for in discarding the Old Testament, he is making a move that the writers of the New Testament themselves would not have endorsed. But perhaps most problematic of all, the preacher was being relationally reckless.

The Things We Keep

When each of my parents passed away, there was a lot of stuff to be gone through. Most folks leave a variety of belongings behind when they die, and the business of sorting through it all becomes part of the grief process for their loved ones. I am a naturally sentimental guy, and so it was a bittersweet sort of a pleasure for me to spend those hours with those things. And the agonizing decision lies in what things to keep and what things to discard.

Here is what I did not do: I did not throw away everything from my parents' lives that came from the time before I was born. Instead, the opposite is true. I find that I especially cherish and learn from those letters, journals, and memorabilia that predate me. I am glad that I kept so many copies of letters that my mother and father wrote to me. But isn't there a chance that I will learn still more about them and understand them better by reading things that they wrote to each other or to other friends or family members? I limit myself and my understanding if I retain only those things from my parents that pertain to me.

The analogy is an imperfect one, to be sure, but you see my point. If the Old Testament people of God were in a relationship with the same God that I am, might I not learn some things about my God from them? Isn't it possible that their relationship with God could enhance and inform mine?

I don't believe that the Old Testament Law is addressed exclusively to the Hebrews of Moses' generation. Rather, I take my cue from Jesus, who said that the Law—even the smallest details of it—will not pass away and should not be discarded. And yet even if I regarded the Law as historically bound, I still would not dismiss it because of this crucial overlap that I share with ancient Israel: their God is my God.

The significance of that overlap is magnified when we consider with whom we are dealing. We believe that God is eternal and unchanging. And if that is true, that makes everything that God has said eternally relevant—perhaps not equally relevant to every situation, but always relevant to knowing and understanding the One who said it.

If, in going through my late father's things, I read something that he wrote when he was fifteen years old, it would be fascinating to me. Yet it would only be a snapshot of him at that age. I could not take it as an unimpeachable insight into his thinking for his entire life.

When we are dealing with God, however, the circumstance is different. "I, the LORD, do not change," God declares (Malachi 3:6). What was an expression of an unchanging God's heart four thousand years ago, therefore, must at all times be an expression of that heart. The circumstances may change, the audience may change, and even the covenant may change, but the God who spoke the word does not.

If I do not have the same God as Moses, then the Mosaic law will be to me only a historical curiosity. But since his God is my God, then what God said to him matters to me. Out of mere fairness to my own relationship with the Lord, therefore, I cannot "just throw out anything that's in the Old Testament."

The Relational Law

The first five books of the Bible—Genesis, Exodus, Leviticus, Numbers, and Deuteronomy—are often grouped together and referred to as "the Law." In terms of the actual material, however, as we have noted earlier, Genesis and the first half of Exodus are devoted not to laws but to stories. The Law material begins in the middle of Exodus. It begins when the people of Israel camp at Mount Sinai. It begins with the Ten Commandments. And the Ten Commandments begin with this statement: "I am the LORD your God, who brought you out of the land of Egypt, out of the house of slavery. You shall have no other gods before Me" (Exodus 20:2-3).

"I am the LORD your God, who . . ." Notice the prominence of "I," "your," and "who," for that is the starting place for the Law. We cannot understand the Law unless we appreciate where it begins, and it begins with a *who*. The Law is deliberately located within the context of a relationship.

We must never read the Law as an impersonal thing, you see. It is not cold and detached. Rather, it is as personal, as relational, as the letters of Paul, the prayers of David, or the love song of Solomon. The Law has a from-me-to-you quality to it. It is spoken and written from a perspective that says, "This is about us!"

We noted earlier that the Ten Commandments were kept in that sacred container known as the ark of the covenant. The Law served as the terms of the covenant between God and the people. And so the very act of placing the tablets representing the Law in a container known as the ark of the covenant is to locate the Law in the context of a relationship.

God's starting place for the Law, therefore, is a marvelously personal one. The Lord does not overwhelm Israel with the divine resume. The starting place is not a statement about what the Lord is in terms of power, glory, majesty, or knowledge. God could have begun there, but did not. Nor is the starting place a statement about who the Lord is in relation to the universe, the heavenly host, the creatures, or the nations. That could have been an impressive preamble, but it's not where God chose to begin. Instead, the self-introduction is a statement about who the Lord is in relation to Israel: "I am the LORD your God, who brought you out of the land of Egypt, out of the house of slavery."

We see a similar intimacy earlier when the Lord first called Moses at Mount Sinai. Evidently, Moses did not yet know the Lord, and so an introduction was required. And we see that God's self-introduction to Moses is, again, personal and relational. "I am the God of your father, the God of Abraham, the God of Isaac, and the God of Jacob" (Exodus 3:6 ESV). The truth, of course, is that the Lord is God of a great deal more than just Abraham, Isaac, and Jacob. And yet, as we see at the beginning of the Ten Commandments, God does not identify God's self in terms of resumé, attributes, or achievements, but in terms of people.

We employ this same sort of sweet, personal instinct with babies. How many new parents or grandparents have held a newborn and introduced themselves? "Do you know who I am?" we ask. And then we proceed to tell the little thing. But we don't bother telling the baby about our career or our awards, our degrees or publications, our salary or net worth. No, we tell the baby who we are to them. "I'm your daddy," we earnestly explain, "and I love you very much."

So, too, the Lord God narrows himself to speak to the people. God does not scratch the surface of saying all that God is. Rather, the Lord says who the Lord is to us. The God who formed human beings and breathed into them, and who came looking for them in Eden; the God who asks questions and initiates covenants; the God who self-reveals in terms of parent, shepherd, and spouse; and the God who says that the greatest commandment is to love—that God is a relational God. Far from the detached Creator of Deism, this God is intimately involved in our lives. And so God's Law begins with *who* and is located in the context of a relationship.

Who God Is to Us

The Law is given in the context of relationship. And our relationships occur in the context of time and space. This comes with the territory of being human, and so it naturally becomes an aspect of our relationship with the Lord. We necessarily relate to God in time and space.

The Lord introduces the Law in terms of relationship, and that relationship is presented at two levels. First, there is what God has been to the people in their past. Then there is what God must be to them in their present and future.

The Lord is not a stranger to this people. There is the profound, long-standing history that God has with them—"the God of your father, the God of Abraham, the God of Isaac, and the God of Jacob." And, too, there is the very recent and memorable history that God has with them—"your God, who brought you out of the land of Egypt, out of the house of slavery." These people have been the beneficiaries of God's choice, call, providence, and deliverance. They have witnessed God's miraculous intervention on their behalf. They have known God's companionship and guidance on their journey to this juncture. And now they experience the awesome presence of the Lord, speaking to them of their mutual relationship.

It is a relationship of time and space. The past on the time line was Egypt on the map. The future on the time line would be Canaan on the map. And their present was being lived in the wilderness. They had seen the work and character of God in their past. They were witnessing God's presence and power in the present. And they were to trust God's promise and purpose for the future.

What was true for Israel at Sinai is true for you and me, as well, at special moments in our experience. Those moments may not have the historic significance of Israel at Sinai, but they are important for us nonetheless. They are those moments where we are prompted to stop where we are and look both ways. We look back with gratitude as we see God's hand and leading. And we look ahead with faith as we trust that same God for an unknown future. This is the precious witness of John Newton. Newton had left the faith of his childhood, becoming a hardened and angry seaman. Eventually, he was a participant in the British slave trade until a storm at sea turned him back to the grace of God. In his famous testimony, when he looked both backward and forward, he saw himself surrounded by that amazing grace. "'Tis grace hath brought me safe thus far," Newton sings, "and grace will lead me home."[1] And Robert Robinson echoed the same sort of look-both-ways testimony. "Hither by thy help I'm come; and I hope, by thy good pleasure, safely to arrive at home."[2]

At the very beginning of any relationship, there is no past to recall, to learn from, or to build upon. Some excitement comes with newness, to be sure, but also a great many unknowns. For the children of Israel at Sinai—and for any of us who have some years and some miles on our walk with God—there is a past. They have experience, familiarity, knowledge. They have a salvation story. And that is the context, then, in which they receive God's Law. It comes from "the LORD your God who . . ."

A Personal Touch

The relational way that God speaks to the people is even more personal than we may realize at first glance. To illustrate what is at stake, let us step aside from the Law for a moment and consider a familiar line from the Book of Psalms for illustrative purposes. The New Revised Standard Version renders the first verse of Psalm 110

1   John Newton, "Amazing Grace," *The United Methodist Hymnal*, 378.
2   Robert Robinson, "Come, Thou Fount of Every Blessing," *The United Methodist Hymnal*, 400.

this way: "The LORD says to my lord, 'Sit at my right hand until I make your enemies your footstool'" (Psalm 110:1 NRSV). In an English translation, the English word *lord* appears twice. In the original Hebrew, however, two entirely different words are used. Our English versions, therefore, clue us into the difference by printing one of the two in all capital letters.

Long ago, devout Jews were so careful not to take God's name in vain that they chose not to take it at all. When reading aloud the Hebrew text, they would not pronounce the name where it appeared, but would substitute in its stead *adonai*, the Hebrew word for *lord*. Consequently, all these generations later, we do not actually know how the Hebrew name of God is pronounced. The traditional speculation for many years was *Jehovah*. More recently, the standard scholarly guess is *Yahweh*.

Whatever the correct pronunciation, most of our English translations of the Bible have followed the old Jewish custom. Where the name appears, we substitute the word *lord*. To make the distinction between the name and the title, however, we print LORD in all capital letters where it represents the name.

In the sample from Psalm 110, therefore, the author recites what the LORD (*Yahweh*) said to his lord (*adonai*). The first occurrence is the name of God. The second occurrence is the title for a sovereign.

And so we see another layer of significance in how God begins in speaking the Law to the people. "I am the LORD your God, who brought you out of the land of Egypt." It is not only highly relational, it is also highly personal. God identifies himself by name.

Recurring Motif

If the Old Testament Law were a piece of classical music, perhaps some of us would be able to listen to it more carefully and hear it more clearly. For when we listen to great and sophisticated music, we are accustomed to listening for motifs, for the way the composer builds on themes, and for the grand interplay of many instruments into a single, majestic piece.

God's Law, I believe, is just as carefully and beautifully composed. The sections are not brass, woodwinds, strings, and percussion, but priests, Levites, people, and nature. Yet what makes this symphony more dramatic is that the Composer also both conducts and plays.

This composition also has its different movements. After the great overture, which is the Ten Commandments, and which introduces so much of what follows, an early movement is devoted to the design and construction of the Tabernacle. Another explores the sacrifices and offerings. Yet another belongs to the holy days. There are also guidelines for commerce, agriculture, warfare, diet, and relationships.

And yet, through every major section of the piece, we hear a recurring motif. What we heard at the very beginning—the first notes played in this great symphony of the Law—we hear woven throughout the entire work. The Law does not just begin with a *who*. *Who* proves to be the central theme of everything that follows as well.

In the midst of instructions to Moses about the Tabernacle and offerings, God explained that the people "shall know that I am the LORD their God who brought them out of the land of Egypt, that I might dwell among them; I am the LORD their God" (Exodus 29:46). Likewise, the people's observance of the "sabbaths" was said to be "a sign between Me and you throughout your generations, that you may know that I am the LORD who sanctifies you" (Exodus 31:13). And the dietary instructions, too, feature this increasingly familiar rationale: "For I am the LORD your God. Consecrate yourselves therefore, and be holy, for I am holy. And you shall not make yourselves unclean with any of the swarming things that swarm on the earth. For I am the LORD who brought you up from the land of Egypt to be your God; thus you shall be holy, for I am holy" (Leviticus 11:44-45).

We keep reading, and we discover that the expression "I am the LORD" appears almost fifty times in just nine chapters of Leviticus. Chapters 18 through 26 include instructions about such disparate matters as sexual relations, idolatry, honoring parents, harvesting fields, loving neighbors, revering the aged, observing holidays, honest business practices, the presentations of offerings, and the conduct of the priests. And that far-flung material is peppered with the reminder of whom they're dealing with: "I am the LORD."

To the casual reader, these expressions of God's self-identification seem randomly scattered throughout the Law. Indeed, they may even come across as unnatural intrusions into the text. The people are not just being introduced to God, after all, so why is God's identity inserted again and again?

And yet that is precisely the point. For the Law is not ultimately about rituals or commerce or sexual ethics or dietary codes. From beginning to end, the Law is about God and the people's relationship to God. To affirm throughout the Law that the LORD is your God is as appropriate—even as lovely—as the inclusion of names in the wedding vows. My obligations and promises as a husband are not made or lived in a vacuum, you see, but in a relationship. "I, David, take thee, Karen . . ."

Furthermore, the reminders of the LORD throughout all the text of the Law becomes a metaphor for the influential presence of the LORD throughout all of life. Israel's God is not just holy on holy days after all. The LORD is not holy only within the precinct of the Tabernacle. Rather, God is holy at all times and in all places. And the people who belong to that God, therefore, are called to be holy at all times and in all places. Or, more to the point, the holiness of their God is meant to percolate through and influence every area of their lives.

The Old Testament Law does have a sense for the distinction between what is holy and what is common, to be sure. But it would be a betrayal of God's nature for God's people to conduct themselves with purity and righteousness only on holy days and in holy places. I would not be pleased, after all, if my wife were only faithful to me on anniversaries and when she was at home.

All of Israel's life—from its high holy days to its most ordinary days; from the sacred celebrations around the altar to the routines of planting and harvesting, cleaning, baking, and eating—was consciously lived before their holy God. The Lord lived in their midst. They were in covenant relationship with him. And so all of life was meant to be lived in continual response to "who."

3
In Praise of the Leash

But those who look into the perfect law, the law of liberty,
and persevere, being not hearers who forget but doers
who act—they will be blessed in their doing.

James 1:25 NRSV

When I was a boy, our family made a trip out to New Jersey to attend the wedding of one of my cousins. While we were there, we spent a good deal of time at my aunt and uncle's house, and I remember being impressed by their dog. In fact, it is that dog, rather than the wedding, that became a lasting memory for me from that weekend.

I don't remember his name anymore, but let's call him Buddy. He made an impression on me at the time for he was so much bigger than the dog we had at home. And as a bigger dog than our toy poodle, he had more energy, needed more exercise, and desired more outdoor time than what I was accustomed to seeing.

Well, my aunt and uncle had a contraption set up for him in their yard. As I recall, it was like a kind of a clothesline attached between two trees. And then there was another line, with a pulley on one end, that ran back and forth along the line between the trees. And that line had an attachment on the other end, which connected to the dog's collar.

Several times a day, they would hook up this big, playful, happy dog to that line, and he would go out and run and jump and frolic and play. He would chase squirrels up the trees, bark at birds, wag his tail at passersby, and when he had tired himself out, he would sleep in the shade.

It was a very happy sight of a very happy dog. And that sight made an impression on me as a kid. It was an impression, in fact, that stayed with me until I was an adult and Karen and I began owning dogs of our own.

Very early in our marriage, we got a dog, whom we named Angel. Don't let the name fool you: he was in no way angelic. He was some sort of terrier, he had all the energy in the world, and I figured he would love being on the kind of run that I had seen at my aunt and uncle's house.

I rigged up a line between two trees, and got Angel all hooked up so he could run. And he liked to run, all right, but he would run full speed to the end of the line, and then get suddenly jerked back when he reached the end. It was awful to see, but he wasn't hurt by it. Neither did he seem to be educated by it, for he kept doing it. In fact, day after day, we'd see the same, silly pattern, until one day, when we weren't watching, he evidently ran so hard that he managed to break his collar off, and he got loose. We never saw him again.

Soon after we lost Angel, we got another dog, whom we named Jewel. We had Jewel for seventeen years. Jewel was not inclined to run away like Angel was, but it turned out that she was no more fond of the contraption in the backyard than he was.

We attached Jewel to that line in the back, figuring that she would enjoy romping and playing in the yard as my aunt and uncle's dog had. But, no, she didn't run. She didn't romp. She didn't play. Instead, Jewel would walk to the extreme edge of the reach of the leash—straining it to the point where it was tugging at her neck—and then she'd lie down there in a kind of quiet protest at the extreme perimeter of the run.

I went for years without thinking much about our failed experiments with a backyard run for our dogs. And then one day, reading the Psalms, I came across a happy exclamation that reminded me of those several dogs. "I run in the path of your commandments, for you have set my heart free" (Psalm 119:32 WEB).

The very appealing image of running and being free reminded me of those three different dogs. I had seen one of them run happily on a long leash. I had seen one of them run in a way that was determined to break free from the leash. And I had seen one of them not run at all, evidently feeling rather oppressed by the leash. Those dogs combine with the psalmist to teach me a lesson about God's Law.

Living Like Angel

The backyard leash serves as a kind of law for the dog. It creates boundaries. It limits movement, to be sure, yet still it is not a cage. It affords the dog a lot of room to run and play, and all the while it protects the dog from getting lost or being endangered by traffic. The three dogs in my experience, however, responded to their leashes in very different ways. And, likewise, different people respond very differently to God's Law.

When I was a youth minister, I remember a girl in my group taking me aside one day to ask me about God's forgiveness. "Will God forgive any sin I have committed?" she asked. I assured her about the magnitude of God's forgiveness, about the "grace that is greater than all our sin!"[1] Then she followed up: "What if I wanted to do it again?" I told her that was to be expected as a part of our sinful nature. Then she smiled embarrassedly, and finally got to what she really wanted to know. "What if I plan on doing it again?"

This is the familiar dilemma of so many believers. They are irresistibly drawn to something that they know is outside the boundaries of the leash. They are like our dog Angel, who was not content to live and play within the confines of our yard. And so he went bolting, headstrong, toward the "freedom" that he craved.

We human beings have a comparable experience. Ours is different from Angel's in that God's Law is much easier to break than a leash. Where our experience mirrors the dog's, however, is that breaking away turns into being lost.

This is the phenomenon embodied by Jesus' cherished story of the prodigal son (Luke 15:11-32). The young man got it in his head that there was something better "out there." For all the beauty and abundance of his father's house, he was determined to leave home and pursue that mirage of pleasure and satisfaction on some horizon. Interestingly, the father did not force the son to stay home. And so it is with God and us. Ever since the garden of Eden, God has entrusted us with the freedom that allows us to disobey—to wander, to endanger ourselves, and even to distance ourselves from the One who made us and loves us. I have no doubt that the father would rather the son stay home, but he does not force the son to stay.

Like so many of us, the prodigal proves to be tragically farsighted. He is unable to see clearly his father and his father's house while he is still living at home. It is only when he is at a great distance that he finally realizes just how good home is. And so he returns, and he is welcomed back by the loving and forgiving embrace of his father.

---

1   Julia H. Johnston, "Grace Greater than Our Sin," *The United Methodist Hymnal*, 365.

Jesus' parable of the prodigal son has a happy ending because the son comes home. But the happy ending mustn't prevent us from recognizing the pain and folly of leaving home in the first place. God's Law marks the boundaries of the Father's property, and we are encouraged to live within that lovely estate. Yet we break the leash and run away, getting miserably and dangerously lost in the process.

Living Like Jewel

Jesus' parable of the prodigal son includes another character. The story is not just about the father and the son who runs away. There is another son, the prodigal's older brother. My dad preached a sermon about him, calling him "the prodigal that stayed at home."

The older brother, you see, did not run away like his younger sibling. Yet still we don't sense in his part of the story that he is the role model for us to emulate. True, he didn't leave home, yet it's clear that his heart is not right. Even if he physically stays in the right place, he was not where he ought to be spiritually.

This is another familiar plight. Grudging obedience hardly qualifies as obedience, at all. Jesus told his disciples, "If you love me, keep my commands" (John 14:15 NIV). The sort of obedience that the Lord desires, you see, is the obedience that flows from love. But joyless, teeth-gritting compliance is hardly pleasing to the heart of God.

Here, then, is evidence of how fundamentally relational God is. If the Lord was emotionally distant from us, then merely keeping the rules would be enough. The highway patrol, after all, doesn't really care whether I am happy as I drive or not, but only whether I am driving safely within the rules of the road.

But God wants more from us than just joyless cooperation. In our human relationships, we take no pleasure in obligatory thank-you notes or thoughtless gifts. Yes, the duty has been done, but not in a way that is relationally satisfying and meaningful. And so, too, the Lord wants more from us than mere acquiescence.

One senses that the Pharisees were prodigals that stayed at home. They had not crossed the boundaries of God's Law in the way that so many whom they condemned as "sinners" had. Yet Jesus does not commend them for their obedience. Rather than living the joyful, grateful, loving existence that would please the Lord, they seemed to be mostly box-checking legalists, who tended to be self-righteous and judgmental. They were the older brothers who stayed at home, but they weren't right on the inside.

I picture our dog Jewel, sitting there at the very edge of the leash, in unhappy protest. She was not running and playing within the safety afforded her by the leash in the backyard. Nor did she boldly break the leash and leave home. No, she just sat there at the edge, uncomfortable and unhappy.

How many believers live their lives miserably on the edges of God's Law? They are not running. They are not happy or free. They are cranky in their compliance. And, ironically, their vision is no better than the prodigal's, for they do not see how good home is either.

Ah, but when we do see how beautiful and abundant is the Father's house, then we will see how good is the Law that keeps us close to home.

Living Like the Psalmist (and Buddy)

Consider for a moment the broad sweep of Israel's salvation story. In Egypt, God gave the people their freedom. In Canaan, God gave them their home. And in between, at Sinai, God gave them the Law.

It's a fascinating flow. Right in between their past life of bondage and their future life of freedom, God gave them the Law. I believe that placement—in both time and space—is deliberate and meaningful, for there is an expressed relationship between the people's liberty and God's Law. Liberty and law go together. For lawlessness, after all, is not freedom, but chaos. Imagine traffic without laws.

So the same God who had so recently manifested a profound desire for his people to be free now helps them guarantee that freedom by giving them the Law. And this, then, is where you and I come in.

Obedience to the Law is not how we are saved, for the Law came after Israel had been saved. God didn't say to the ancient Israelites while they were still in Egypt, "Here are my commandments. If you obey them, then I'll set you free." No, God set them free and then gave them the commandments. God's Law is for free people. God's Law is for people who are already saved.

Naturally, the people welcomed their freedom from bondage as a gift from God. A generation later, the people rejoiced in the Promised Land as a gift from God. And in between, the wise ones embraced the Law also as a gift from God.

The psalmist knew the Law was a good thing just as my aunt and uncle's dog knew the leash was a good thing.

God has set us free and then prescribed for us in the Law the boundaries within which we may freely run. They are boundaries that keep us from danger. They keep us from being lost. They keep us from chaos. They are boundaries that keep us in right relationship with God and in right relationship with other people. They keep us faithful, pure, and fulfilled. God sets us free to live happily, safely, and robustly within those boundaries.

The dog that I met at my aunt and uncle's house made an impression on me as a boy. And after I had grown up, I learned from the dog's example. I thought that my dogs should be just like him. But I was wrong. For the psalmist has taught me that it wasn't about my dogs; it was about me. I am the one who "runs in the path of God's commands, for he has set my heart free."

4
Looking for the Expiration Date

"You shall not add to the word which I am commanding
you, nor take away from it, that you may keep the
commandments of the LORD your God which I command
you."

Deuteronomy 4:2

My wife, Karen, grew up in a family full of milk drinkers. In addition to her and her folks, she grew up with three brothers, and everyone's glass of milk was filled and refilled each dinner hour. As a result, milk never had a chance to go bad in her house.

In my house, on the other hand, there were not so many of us, and we were not such big milk drinkers. A gallon of milk was more likely to have a long life in our refrigerator, and so we were careful about checking the expiration date. Also, my mom would often smell the milk before pouring just to confirm that it was still good.

Well, one day when Karen and I were both young and just dating, she was at our house as I was pouring myself a bowl of cereal. After I poured the milk, I was suspicious that it had soured, and so I asked her to taste it for me to see if it seemed fine to her. But coming from the home she did, she was completely naive about what she was about to put in her mouth.

I can still picture her draped over the kitchen sink, running the water across her poor, surprised tongue.

So it is that human beings want to have nothing to do with something that is expired. Once a thing is expired, you see—milk, a credit card, a parking meter, or what have you—it is of no use or value to us.

The question for us to consider, then, is whether the Old Testament Law is expired.

Did the Law Expire with Jesus?

The most common reasoning I have seen on this point is the assumption that the Law has nothing to do with us because it is "Old Testament" and we are "New Testament." Folks with this view believe that the Old Testament Law has been rendered irrelevant because of Christ.

The great irony of that position, of course, is that it runs so contrary to what Christ himself said. It was Jesus—not Moses in the Old Testament or some Pharisee in the New Testament—who said, "Until heaven and earth pass away, not the smallest letter or stroke shall pass away from the Law, until all is accomplished" (Matthew 5:18). It was Jesus, not Moses or a Pharisee, who went on to say, "Anyone who sets aside one of the least of these commandments and teaches others accordingly will be called least in the kingdom of heaven, but whoever practices and teaches these commands will be called great in the kingdom of heaven" (Matthew 5:19 NIV).

As we continue then to read Jesus' teachings in the Sermon on the Mount, we discover more fully his attitude toward the Law. He cites, for example, the commandment not to kill. Most of us don't come any nearer to breaking that commandment than we do becoming Knights of the Round Table. But then Jesus presses the matter further. He talks about being angry with another person, putting that very common experience in the same camp with killing.

Likewise, Jesus cites the commandment not to commit adultery. This is a sin that some avoid out of genuine love and faithfulness, others out of purity and godliness, and a great many others out of little more than fear. But then Jesus raises the stakes. "I say to you that everyone who looks at a woman with lust has already committed adultery with her in his heart" (Matthew 5:28 NRSV). Suddenly, the number of adulterers has increased exponentially.

Is this, then, the new way that we are to look at the Old Testament Law because we are followers of Christ? Rather than dismissing it or defusing it, Jesus intensifies and personalizes it. For as long as the Law is simply a set of behavioral boundaries I must not cross, I might stand a fair chance of staying out of foul territory. But Jesus teaches me that it isn't only my behavior, it's my heart.

On one occasion, the Pharisees, who were increasingly antagonistic toward Jesus, tried to find fault with him by pointing out something his disciples had done wrong. The Pharisees were fastidious about following certain procedures—notably external ones—with respect to hand washing before eating. They observed that the disciples had failed to do this, and they criticized Jesus for it. Jesus turned the issue inside out, however, explaining that it's not what goes into our mouths that defiles us but what comes out of our mouths. What goes into our mouths, he notes, simply goes through the digestive system. But what comes out of our mouths originates in the heart—things like deceit, pride, envy, and foolishness—and those are the things that truly defile a person (Mark 7:15-23).

It is no wonder, then, that Jesus called his followers to a righteousness that was greater than the scribes' and the Pharisees'. The scribes were the folks in that time and place who were expert in the Law of God. And the Pharisees were the people renowned for their careful obedience to that Law. Yet Jesus insisted, "Unless your righteousness surpasses that of the Pharisees and the teachers of the law, you will certainly not enter the kingdom of heaven" (Matthew 5:20 NIV).

The Pharisees emphasized external obedience, while missing the heart of the matter. And in our day, we have a new form of Pharisaism, which operates as a kind of "no harm, no foul" ethic. The external-versus-internal dichotomy of the Pharisees' day has morphed into a public-versus-private way of evaluating morality in our day. If no one is harmed by my behavior, the reasoning goes, then what makes it bad? C. S. Lewis said it is like a captain of a ship concluding that "it does not matter what his ship is like on the inside provided that he does not run into the next ship."[1] Jesus is insistent, however, that it matters immensely what we are like on the inside.

As I reflect on the teachings of Jesus, therefore, I cannot conclude that the Law expired with him. Quite the contrary. I am led to believe that the Law was the 101-level course, and now he is pushing me further and deeper. The things we learned in that elementary material are not discarded but built upon. And so the teachings of Jesus do not set aside the Law, but build upon it.

Did Jesus Wave Off the Law?

The Pharisees were widely admired in their day. They were known for their careful religiosity. They were notoriously devout. Yet they don't have a very favorable reputation in our day, primarily owing to the fact that most of what you and I know of the Pharisees comes from Jesus' critiques of them.

---

1   C. S. Lewis, *Mere Christianity* (Harper: San Francisco, 1980), 72.

The irony is that some of what we think we know about Jesus comes from the Pharisees' critiques of him.

On several occasions, the Pharisees accused Jesus of breaking the Sabbath law. Each time, Jesus defended his actions (or, in one instance, his disciples' actions). And those encounters leave many of us with the impression that Jesus was dismissive of the Sabbath commandment. We inadvertently buy into the Pharisees' analysis without giving careful attention to Jesus' interpretation.

The Sabbath commandment prohibits working on the Sabbath day, but it does not define what "work" is. Years of traditions had accumulated between the days of Moses and the days of Jesus, and so the Pharisees had a highly proscriptive definition of what it looked like to honor the Sabbath. Almost no activity was permissible. And so, when they saw Jesus heal on the Sabbath, they condemned him for it.

We must bear in mind, however, that the stories are not of Jesus and his disciples cleaning the fishing nets on the Sabbath or planting a field or building a house. He healed. And he demonstrated to his accusers the rightness of his actions (Matthew 12:11-12; Mark 3:4; Luke 13:15-16). His thesis was not that the Sabbath law could be disregarded, but rather that his behavior was consistent with the spirit of the Sabbath law.

Meanwhile, on another occasion, a Pharisee, who was also a scribe, tested Jesus with a question: "Teacher, which is the great commandment in the Law?" (Matthew 22:36). And Jesus famously responded by citing two commandments from the Old Testament Law. From Deuteronomy, he quoted the command to love God with all we are. And from Leviticus, he quoted the commandment to love one's neighbor as one's self. And then he concluded, "On these two commandments depend the whole Law and the Prophets" (Matthew 22:40).

That summary statement has tempted many Christians to suspect that the Law has been nullified by Jesus' simplification of it. "You don't have to bother with all of those chapters and chapters of details," we imagine Jesus saying, "so long as you love God and neighbor." And thus the bulk of the Law is waved off.

The so-called Golden Rule elicits a similar reaction from many. "So in everything, do to others what you would have them do to you," Jesus said, "for this sums up the Law and the Prophets" (Matthew 7:12 NIV). There it is, then. Because the one rule sums up the rest, we are tempted to think that it replaces the rest.

We would not think it sufficient for the coach of a basketball team to say to the players, "Score more points than the other guys." It would be fair to remark that such an instruction sums up all of the coaching, the designed plays, the offensive and defensive strategies, and such. But to sum them up is not to disregard them. On the contrary, as soon as I understand that the whole purpose is to score more points than the other team, I should naturally want to ask, "How best can we do that?" And then the coach will remind me of all of the things we covered in practice.

Jesus keeps before our eyes the real purpose of the Law. Lest we get lost in a roundabout of fussy religiosity, he keeps us pointed in the right direction. It's about loving God and loving neighbor, nothing less. But as soon as I am reminded of the real point, I will earnestly ask, "What does that look like to love God? How am I to go about loving my neighbor?" And then I may turn to the Law for instruction.

This is the principle that John Calvin called "the third use of the Law," which he regarded as the primary importance of the Law for the Christian. "It is the best instrument for enabling [us] daily to learn with greater truth and certainty what that will of the Lord is which [we] aspire to follow."[2]

The actions and the teachings of Jesus, then, do not dismiss the Law, but invite us back into it.

---

2   John Calvin, The Institutes of the Christian Religion, II.vii.12

Did Jesus Fulfill the Law?

"Do not think," Jesus said, "that I have come to abolish the Law or the Prophets" (Matthew 5:17 NIV). Yet that is precisely what so many Christians do think. It is because of Jesus, they reckon, that we may ignore the Old Testament Law. It has reached its expiration date in him.

But Jesus explains that his achievement with respect to the Law is a different one. He continues, "I have not come to abolish . . . but to fulfill." Our first task, then, should not be to look for the expiration date, but rather to look for the fulfillment date. Let us not ponder which parts of the Law have expired, but which parts of the Law have been fulfilled.

Fulfillment is a great refrain throughout the four Gospels. Fourteen different times, Jesus or one of the Gospel writers refers to some scripture being fulfilled. And, likewise, the New Testament letter to the Hebrews sees in Jesus the fulfillment of so much of the Law.

Jesus is our great High Priest and our Paschal Lamb. He is the offering without blemish and the once-for-all atoning sacrifice. He is the serpent hung on a pole and the scapegoat that carries off the sins of the people. He goes behind the veil into the Holy of Holies, and it is his blood that is sprinkled as cleansing, as sanctification, and as the blood of the new covenant.

Jesus does not come to abolish the Law of God but to fulfill it. He fulfills its types and figures. And he fulfills its righteous demands.

Now someone says, "Isn't this really just a matter of semantics? Isn't this a distinction without a difference? After all, what does it matter whether we say the Law is 'expired' or say that the Law is 'fulfilled'? Either way, we don't have to worry about the Law anymore. The end result is the same in either case."

No, I don't think so. For a thing that is expired, you see, is a thing that has become no longer good. A thing that is fulfilled, on the other hand, is a thing that has become "more good." The Law has not become irrelevant for us because of Christ; it has become better for us because of Christ.

The Case of the Credit Card

And so we return to the basic, practical question: Are you and I, as Christians, still obliged to obey the Old Testament Law?

Let's say that I have a credit card, on which the embossed expiration date is this month three years from now. I take that card with me into a store today to make a purchase. Imagine, though, that when I present the card for payment, the clerk returns it to me and says, "I'm sorry, I can't accept this card because it's expired."

I'm surprised and puzzled at first, and so I take the card back. After looking at it again, though, I reply to the clerk, "No, no, it doesn't expire for three more years!" I direct her attention to the date on the card.

"Yes, I know that's what the card says," she matter-of-factly responds, "but I say that it is expired now!"

That would be ridiculous, of course. It is not the prerogative of a random clerk in a store to tell me that my credit card has expired. The expiration date can only be set by the entity that issued the card.

And that is a fundamental principle for us to recognize, both with respect to the Old Testament Law, in particular, and in regard to the larger whole of Scripture, in general. The only One who is eligible to say that any part of the Law—or any part of the Bible, for that matter—is expired is the One who issued it.

It is commonplace in mainline American Christianity, however, for us to take that prerogative for ourselves. Frankly, it would be amusing if it weren't so serious. And our guiding principle is equally amusing, and fairly transparent. Simply put: we tend to edit out of Scripture the parts we don't like.

Bishop C. FitzSimons Allison argues that there is an innate selfishness in every heresy. "Each heresy," he writes, "in its own way encourages some flaw in our human nature."[3] If he is correct, then we must be vigilant about the ulterior motives that may drive some of our interpretation of Scripture, including the widespread tendency to ignore the parts we don't like or that make us uncomfortable.

I suppose it was all right, when I was a little boy, for my mother to cut the crust off of my bread because I didn't like that part. It is not all right, however, for me as an adult to cut off parts of the Bible because I don't like them. The only one who can say that some part of the Law is expired is the One who issued it. That's not me, and it's not you. And I expect that it's not our culture either.

From the New Testament on, Christians have understood that certain parts of the Law have been fulfilled. They—the rituals, the symbols, the blood—point us to Christ. And since Christ has come, we no longer need to settle for his antecedents. We may simply rejoice in them and be edified by them in the same way we are by the symbols that may adorn our sanctuaries. (We will explore this truth in greater detail in the chapter on the Tabernacle.)

Likewise, we know from Scripture that God has established a new covenant with a new people. And some of the signs and practices, which were meant to identify the Old Testament people of God—like circumcision or the dietary code—are no longer applied to the New Testament people of God. Now we have other signs and practices that identify us, like baptism and Communion.

And therein lies the key to better understanding our relationship to the Old Testament Law. Some particulars change from Old Testament to New, from Israel to the church, from Law to Gospel. Some particulars change, but the principles remain. That is the truth we will unpack together in the next chapter.

---

3   C. FitzSimons Allison, *The Cruelty of Heresy* (New York: Morehouse Publishing, 1994), 23.

In the meantime, we would do well to remind ourselves of the psalmist's high view of the Law. Psalm 119, for example, is the longest chapter in the Bible, and that psalm is mostly a prayer that praises and thanks God for the Law. Even apart from reading the psalm, the very fact of its length and subject is instructive to us. If we were told that the longest chapter in the Bible was an expression of gratitude to God for something, what might we imagine that something was? I expect we'd make a pretty long list before coming to the Law.

How often do we praise God for the Law? We praise and thank the Lord for the beauty and glory of creation, the mighty works of God in the past, the saving work of God in our lives, the blessings we have known, or the very attributes of God himself. But how often do we praise God for the Law?

The psalmist understood that those who live according to the Law are happy, that God's instructions are a source of pleasure and wisdom, and that the teachings of the Law give freedom. The psalmist says that the Law is worth more than earthly treasures, that it is perfect, and that it is eternal.

It is not milk, you see. It does not go bad.

5
Understanding the Speed Limit

*"Therefore every teacher of the law who has become a
disciple in the kingdom of heaven is like the owner of a
house who brings out of his storeroom new treasures as
well as old."*

Matthew 13:52 NIV

My drive between home and church takes about twenty minutes,
and during that drive the speed limit changes nearly a dozen times.
The big, white SPEED LIMIT sign reads 25, then 35 a little while down
the road . . . all the way up to 70 at some point.

The range of speed limits within a mere twenty-minute drive does
not upset us. We are not flummoxed by the inconsistency, nor are we
bewildered by the mixed messages. Rather, it makes perfect sense to
us that a residential road would limit drivers' speed to twenty-five
miles per hour, while an interstate highway affords those same
drivers the freedom to go seventy miles per hour.

We understand from both instinct and experience the phenomenon of speed limit signs. They have both an element that is constant and an element that is changing. The constant element is the underlying principle expressed by the words on each sign. The principle is that, whatever road you may be on, there is a maximum speed that is safe for traffic on that road. The varying element, meanwhile, is the actual number. What that maximum safe speed is, after all, depends upon the context. In our study of the Old Testament Law, we ought to keep a speed limit sign before our eyes.

Strolling Through the Museum

I have enjoyed the privilege of traveling to the Holy Land on a half-dozen different occasions. And while there, I have heard stories about the important role that archaeology plays in the modern state of Israel. "You can hardly build a new road or dig the foundation for a new building," one tour guide told us, "without uncovering some ancient artifact. And so the workers have to stop what they're doing so that the experts can come in and evaluate what they've found."

A trip through a museum in almost any of the countries of the Near East, as well as a tour of so many excavated sites in that part of the world, features a treasury of ancient artifacts. Here is a tool from the time of this Israelite king or papyri from that Egyptian dynasty. Here is an Ammonite knife, a piece of Babylonian art, an Aramean pot.

So let us imagine ourselves walking through a museum, and we come across a glass case displaying eating utensils, cups, and bowls from the Early Bronze Age. We gaze at them with fascination, recognizing that this was the stuff of life for Abraham and Sarah. Our imaginations transport us back to the times and stories, the people and places that we learned about in Sunday school.

Perhaps this is the sort of pot Jacob used when he made the stew that Esau found irresistible. Perhaps this is the kind of cup that Sarah brought out as hospitality to those three heavenly visitors. We are fascinated by such objects. And yet we do not fancy the idea of taking them home and using them in our kitchens and dining rooms. I have not yet met a Christian who contends that because a certain sort of utensil was used by Abraham, Moses, or David, it ought also to be used by us today. Yet the Old Testament Law is different. It is more than an ancient artifact, more than a historical curiosity.

Our endeavor in this book is not merely to come to an arm's-length appreciation of the Old Testament Law. We don't hold it at a distance like a four-thousand-year-old cup. Rather, unlike that cup, we want to bring the Law into our homes, we want to use it in our daily lives. Why? Because we embrace the Law with the confidence that the God who gave it in Moses' day is the same God we serve in our day. And if that be so, then the Law has as much meaning and relevance for us as it did for its first audience at Sinai.

Yet we struggle to know how to employ it and apply it. Someone has translated the language of the Law for us from ancient Hebrew into modern English. Can someone also translate the content of the Law for us from the ancient Near East to the twenty-first-century West?

Modern Signs and Ancient Laws

Too often Christians fall into one of two traps. The one trap is to try to carry the entire Old Testament Law into our contemporary living. The other trap is to try to dismiss entirely the Old Testament Law as though it was nothing to do with contemporary living.

The group that falls into the former trap is commendably earnest. The members of this group have a high regard for Scripture, so they endeavor to take virtually all of the Law and impose it onto our lives today. Their rationale is that it's biblical; therefore, it is meant for us.

Another group of believers, meanwhile, tends toward a different approach. They toss out virtually all of the Law, arguing that it was from and for a different context, and so it does not apply to us. For them, the Law is more like the four-thousand-year-old cup in the museum—interesting, but not suitable for today's kitchens.

The first group is reverently protective of Scripture, but they tend to be suspicious of the human capacity and responsibility for application. The latter group is very confident in human interpretation and application, but they may be reckless with Scripture. I believe the best solution lies between those two extremes.

And so we return to our image of the speed limit sign, an indicator so familiar to American drivers that they only feature two elements—words and numbers. The words are always the same. The numbers vary from road to road.

The words represent a principle, and that principle is unchanging. The principle is that, on any given road, there is a maximum safe speed. To exceed that speed, therefore, is against the law.

The numbers, meanwhile, represent the application of the principle, and the application varies. The maximum safe speed on my residential street is quite different from the maximum safe speed on the interstate highway. Yet while the application of the principle varies from the one road to the other, the principle applies to both.

You and I travel a different road than Moses and his people did. It seems likely, therefore, that our speed limit, if you will, would be different from theirs. Yet we still must have a speed limit. To borrow the "numbers" from Moses' signs would be to ignore the importance of context. But to throw out the "words" would be to live recklessly.

Our endeavor, therefore, is to distinguish the words from the numbers, to be able to differentiate between the principle and the application of the principle.

Double Check

When I arrived at the airport for a recent overseas trip, I used my passport at an automated kiosk to check my baggage. I had to show that passport again a few minutes later when acquiring my boarding pass. Then I was asked to produce it yet another time when going through security. And then, one more time, they asked to see my passport at the gate where I boarded the plane.

In settings where we are careful, you see, we make sure to double-check things. "Measure twice and cut once" is the sage wisdom of the workshop. And the teller at the bank counts out the cash I am withdrawing and then a second time aloud in front of me as a double check.

Certainly the Bible deserves such carefulness from us as well. How we interpret Scripture and apply it to our lives ought to benefit from a thoughtful double check. And when it comes to the Old Testament Law, we have an excellent tool to assist us: the New Testament.

As we have noted above, many folks carelessly assume that the New Testament contravenes the Old Testament. They suspect that, as "new" is opposite of "old," so the two testaments are somehow opposed to each other. Yet that is an ironic and risky misunderstanding of both sections of Scripture. New Testament writers themselves would not have endorsed such a bifurcation.

My mother had a saying. I don't think it originated with her, but she is the one I heard say it so many times when I was a child. "The New is in the Old concealed; the Old is in the New revealed." The two testaments are partners, not adversaries. And so we may employ the New Testament, not as an excuse to ignore the Old Testament Law, but as a tool for understanding and applying that Law to our lives.

A few examples will help us illustrate the point.

Israel's Camp

I heard a story years ago about a man who lost his sight, and so he had to learn how to navigate his way through life without the benefit of vision. In his home, he learned exactly where everything was so that he could move about easily and function very naturally in that daily environment. And then, after a few years, he had a vacation home built near a lake that he loved, and it was constructed to be an exact duplicate of his primary residence so that his daily pattern would remain familiar.

Israel's camp had something of the same feel. The Lord had given the people specific directions for the arrangement of their campsite as they journeyed through the wilderness. And those instructions indicate that they were to set up their camp the same way wherever they were. So no matter where they happened to be in the territory between Egypt and Canaan, everything was still in the same place for them: the Tabernacle in the center, the priests camped around it, and each of the tribes pitched their tents in their regular, assigned locations.

Israel's campsite, therefore, while vast, was clearly defined. They operated with a clear sense of what was within the camp and what was outside of the camp. And in the Old Testament Law, we read many references to putting someone or something outside of the camp.

The person diagnosed with a contagious skin disease, for instance, was required to live outside the Israelite camp (Leviticus 13:46), and later we see that standard applied to Miriam herself (Numbers 12:15). That treatment was not for lepers alone; the same sort of instruction was applied to those who had become ritually unclean because of certain discharges or contact with a corpse (see Numbers 5:2-3, 31:19; Deuteronomy 23:10). Capital punishment was to be enforced "outside the camp" (for example, Numbers 15:35). Certain elements of animal offerings were not meant for the altar, so those were to be carried outside the camp (for example, Exodus 29:14; Leviticus 4:21). And the people were also instructed to have their bowel movements outside the camp (Deuteronomy 23:12-14).

Taken one at a time, none of these injunctions seems particularly inspiring. Taken all together, however, they combine to reveal a principle. The place where the congregation of God camps is the place where God dwells. And that place, therefore, must be kept pure.

The principle revealed in the details of the Old Testament Law pulses through the New Testament as well.

Jesus taught his disciples about preserving the fellowship among his followers. If one of them sinned against another, the sin was not to be ignored or swept under the rug. Rather, Jesus says, "Go and point out their fault, just between the two of you" (Matthew 18:15 NIV), hopeful that the offending brother will respond and the fellowship be restored. But what if he doesn't respond? Then "take one or two others along, so that 'every matter may be established by the testimony of two or three witnesses'" (v. 16). If he continues to resist, the circle expands: "tell it to the church" (v. 17). "If they still refuse to listen even to the church, treat them as you would a pagan or a tax collector." The goal is purity, you see: getting rid of the sin and brokenness within the community. Redemption is the first, second, and third effort. But if the offending person is recalcitrant, the necessary step for purity is ostracism: to put him outside the camp.

The Apostle Paul echoes the same principle and application when addressing the case of a sinful member in the Corinthian church. "It is actually reported that there is sexual immorality among you, and of a kind that is not found even among pagans," Paul laments. And what is to be done in such a case? "Should you not rather have mourned, so that he who has done this would have been removed from among you?" (1 Corinthians 5:1-2 NRSV). The impurity was not to remain in the midst of the people, you see. The offender was, in effect, to be put out of the camp.

At the end of the New Testament, Revelation offers the ultimate picture of God's perfect plan and place. We are told that the New Jerusalem will be the setting where the Lord will dwell among his people (Revelation 21:2-3), and then we read a list of the things that will not be found in that place. No more death, mourning, or pain will be there (v. 4). And "the cowardly and unbelieving and abominable and murderers and immoral persons and sorcerers and idolaters and all liars" will not be in that city (v. 8). All that is impure, you see, is meant to be "outside the camp."

The "speed limit" in this case, you see, is the principle that where God's people dwell is where God dwells, and that place must be kept pure. We have observed how the application of that principle looks in several different contexts: animal sacrifices, contagious diseases, church discipline. But what does that "speed limit" look like in your daily life and mine?

Paul helps us to understand that God still dwells among his people. The image is just as spatial as the Tabernacle in the midst of Israel's campsite, but it is even more personal for us than it was for them. "Do you not know," Paul asks, "that your body is a temple of the Holy Spirit who is in you?" (1 Corinthians 6:19).

It's an astonishing assertion. The individual believer's physical body becomes a dwelling place for the Spirit of God. And the implications of that are just what we should expect them to be based on the principle we have seen established in the Old Testament Law about the places where God and God's people dwell. The emphasis is on purity. "Flee immorality," Paul exhorts. As he says in chapter 6, "The body is not for immorality, but for the Lord, and the Lord is for the body . . . Therefore glorify God in your body."

Thus we see what the speed limit is on the road that you and I drive today.

Xenophobia?

We know this from the newspapers, from history, and from our own experience: any human being who is high profile and influential is likely to have their critics and is almost certain to be misunderstood—or misrepresented—along the way. It should not surprise us, therefore, that the Old Testament Law also has its critics and has often been misunderstood through the years.

A common point of friction is the Law's attitude toward foreigners. The critics claim that the Law is ruthless and inhospitable in its treatment of foreigners. The perception is that the ancient nation of Israel was encouraged—even commanded—to be prejudiced and xenophobic.

This is, in my judgment, a careless reading of the material. And it overlooks the culture of generosity and hospitality toward the alien and stranger that is engendered in the Law. The people were commanded to welcome the stranger into their midst (Deuteronomy 31:12), to treat him with love and compassion (Deuteronomy 10:19), and to attend to his welfare (Leviticus 23:22; Deuteronomy 14:28-29) and justice (Numbers 35:15; Deuteronomy 24:17, 27:19). The alien was accorded the same Sabbath rest as the people of Israel (Exodus 20:9-10) and was included in Israel's worship of God (Numbers 15:14-16; Deuteronomy 26:10-11).

There are harsher elements in the Law with respect to foreigners. Of course there are. There are harsher elements in the Law with respect to the children of Israel too. It is impossible to create laws in a fallen world without some harshness being built into them, for those laws must both prohibit evil and punish wrongdoing. And so we must not be naively put off by some of the hard words found in the Law. But the hard words regarding foreigners are not rooted in unkindness. For the underlying issue is not racial, but spiritual.

In later practice, it may be that Israel devolved into a merely ethnic distinction between Jews and Gentiles. In the Lord's original design, however, the issue was not race but relationship. Israel had been invited into a covenant with God, while the surrounding nations and peoples served other gods.

The caution built into the Law, therefore, was to establish a kind of a one-way valve of influence between Israel and other peoples. Israel could welcome others into their midst, and thereby into a knowledge of God and God's ways. But what the Law carefully guarded against was an influence flowing in the other direction. The concern was that the peoples who did not know the Lord would lead God's own people astray.

Accordingly, Israel was warned about making covenants with the inhabitants of the land (Exodus 23:32) and taught to be intolerant of their idolatry (Exodus 34:13-15; Deuteronomy 12:2-3). The people of Israel were not to learn from or imitate the other peoples' practices (Deuteronomy 12:30-31; 18:9-14). The Law was cautious about the presence of those who did not know the Lord in the midst of God's people lest they become a snare to them (Exodus 34:12; Deuteronomy 7:16).

This was not paranoia or unwarranted protectionism. The facts of history proved the wisdom of God's Law. For a generation after Moses' death, "The sons of Israel did evil in the sight of the LORD and served the Baals, and they forsook the LORD, the God of their fathers, who had brought them out of the land of Egypt, and followed other gods from *among* the gods of the peoples who were around them, and bowed themselves down to them" (Judges 2:11-12). And, again: "The sons of Israel lived among the Canaanites, the Hittites, the Amorites, the Perizzites, the Hivites, and the Jebusites; and they took their daughters for themselves as wives, and gave their own daughters to their sons, and served their gods" (Judges 3:5-6).

When we get to the New Testament, we see the chief priests legalistically clinging to superficial, ethnic distinctions (John 18:28), and we recognize that the Lord was tearing down those kinds of walls (for example, Acts 10:28; Romans 10:12-13; Ephesians 2:11-16). Yet we mustn't misunderstand what is and what is not being changed in the New Testament. The number on the speed limit sign is changed for the new context, but the fundamental principle remains in force. The principle was never about race but relationship, and the principle still holds.

The Apostle Paul, for example, warns the Corinthians about marrying unbelievers. His language is strong, but it serves to reiterate the fundamental point. "Do not be bound together with unbelievers," he writes, "for what partnership have righteousness and lawlessness, or what fellowship has light with darkness? Or what harmony has Christ with Belial, or what has a believer in common with an unbeliever? Or what agreement has the temple of God with idols? For we are the temple of the living God; just as God said, 'I will dwell in them and walk among them; And I will be their God, and they shall be My people'" (2 Corinthians 6:14-16).

Paul is the first to insist that salvation in Christ extends to the Gentiles as well as the Jews. His marriage counsel, therefore, is not an ethnic protectionism. It is for the New Testament Christians as it was for Old Testament nation of Israel: a distinction between those who do and those who do not know the Lord.

Peter is conscious, too, of the lifestyle differences between the believers and the unbelievers. Recalling how the Christians in his audience once lived, he wrote, "You have spent enough time in the past doing what pagans choose to do—living in debauchery, lust, drunkenness, orgies, carousing and detestable idolatry. They are surprised that you do not join them in their reckless, wild living, and they heap abuse on you" (1 Peter 4:3-4 NIV).

For the Apostle John, the distinction is understood as between those belonging to Christ and those belonging to the world. Accordingly, he urges the believers in his care, "Do not love the world nor the things in the world. If anyone loves the world, the love of the Father is not in him" (1 John 2:15).

John no doubt learned that paradigm from Jesus himself, who told his followers that he had chosen them "out of the world" (John 15:19), and thus they could expect that the world would hate them. Yet for all of that, Jesus does not pray for his followers to be removed from the hostile world (17:15), but rather sends them into it just as he was sent into it (3:16, 20:21). And thus we see that the principle established in the Law remains in full effect in the New Testament: the Lord's eagerness for those who know him to bring others into that relationship, while guarding God's people from becoming like the world around them.

In His Image

In the second chapter of this book, we noted the fundamentally relational quality of the Old Testament Law. God's instructions were not detached pieces of good advice. They were guidelines for living in the context of a relationship. And, specifically, it was a relationship between the people of Israel and their holy God. More than any other theme or principle, the holiness of God is the "speed limit" sign that is spread across the landscape of the Law. Their worship, their diets, their calendar, their commerce, their sexual relations—all of Israelite life was meant to be an extension of the fact that they belonged to a holy God.

Yet there is a surprising additional layer to this theme. The holiness of God was meant to engender a holy people. And I say that is a surprising layer because I'm not sure that we would assume such a connection with many other attributes.

For a slave to serve a wealthy master, for example, hardly implies that the slave will also be wealthy. For an employee to work for a muscular employer does not guarantee that the employee will become muscular. And for a people to belong to an omniscient God does not suggest that those people will themselves be omniscient.

Yet holiness—the most exclusively divine of attributes—was meant to be transferable. Because their God was holy, the people were called to be holy. "Consecrate yourselves therefore," the Lord says to them, "and be holy; for I am holy" (Leviticus 11:44).

At its best, you see, the holiness of the people's lives was not solely an external thing. It played itself out in all sorts of external ways, to be sure, but that was not where it resided. The Lord was looking for a more thoroughgoing holiness. The people were not merely to do things consistent with holiness; they were to *be* holy.

Here, again, we emerge from the Law with a principle—much like the "speed limit"—which is meant to apply in every context of life. Again, we see that the principle found in the Law is confirmed when we double-check it with the New Testament. And the remarkable principle is that the Lord wants us to be like him.

Jesus makes the matter clear in the context of the teacher-disciple relationship. "It is enough for the disciple that he become as his teacher, and the slave like his master" (Matthew 10:25). He also tells a story to illustrate that we are meant to forgive the way God forgives (Matthew 18:23-35). He teaches us to model our treatment of others after God's indiscriminate generosity toward humankind (Matthew 5:43-48). And, at the Last Supper, Jesus gives his followers a "new commandment." It is a commandment to love, which at first blush does not seem all that new. But then we discover that the new element is that they are to love like him. "A new commandment I give to you, that you love one another, even as I have loved you, that you also love one another" (John 13:34).

In recent decades, the initials WWJD have become a familiar guideline for Christian living. The question that the initials raise— What Would Jesus Do?—is just a restatement of a principle that goes back to the Old Testament Law. The principle was that the people of God were to be like the God whom they served. And asking ourselves in every circumstance of life what Jesus would do is simply a means to that same, beautiful end.

6
Because of the Hardness of Your Hearts

"And I will take the heart of stone out of their flesh and give them a heart of flesh, that they may walk in My statutes and keep My ordinances and do them. Then they will be My people, and I shall be their God."

Ezekiel 11:19-20

We don't get very far into the Gospel story before the religious leaders of Jesus' day prove to be a disappointment. The chief priests and scribes prove to be knowledgeable but obtuse in the face of Christmas (Matthew 2:4-10). The Pharisees and Sadducees are scolded from the start by John the Baptist (Matthew 3:7-12). And when Jesus appears on the scene as an adult, the various religious leaders appear to be critical spectators on the fringes of Jesus' ministry while the great mass of people is enthusiastically drawing near to him.

It isn't long, then, before the chief priests, scribes, Pharisees, and Sadducees show themselves to be the antagonists in the story. They hound Jesus, looking for him to take a misstep (Luke 6:6-7), deliberately misunderstanding him and his work (Matthew 12:22-24), complaining about things he said (Mark 2:3-7) and did (Luke 13:10-14), finding fault with his disciples (Mark 7:1-5), and peppering him with questions to challenge him (Matthew 22:15). And in the end, as we recall, those religious leaders are central to the plot to have Jesus arrested and crucified.

Within that context, then, we read the episode in Mark 10. Some of the Pharisees came to Jesus and, according to Mark, they tried to test him by asking about the legality of divorce. Rather than answering their question directly, though, Jesus turned the question back on them. "What did Moses command you?" he asked, referring back to the Old Testament Law. They answered that Moses permitted a man to divorce a woman simply by giving her a written certificate of divorce and sending her away. Then Jesus replied, "Because of your hardness of heart he wrote you this commandment" (Mark 10:5).

Jesus went on to challenge his male audience's thinking about marriage and divorce. He pointed them back to God's design, as revealed in Eden, to illustrate God's perfect will. And he dramatically reinterpreted the meaning of adultery.

For our purposes just now, though, I want us to focus on just the initial line from Jesus' answer. "Because of your hardness of heart (Moses) wrote you this commandment." In one sentence, Jesus paints a fascinating picture of Moses, of the Law, and of his audience.

Every Generation, One Audience

We don't know the exact dates of Moses' birth and death, but we know that he lived and died more than a millennium before Jesus' earthly ministry. The people for whom Moses wrote and the people to whom Jesus spoke, therefore, were separated by over a thousand years. Yet Jesus blends the two audiences together into one. "Because of your hardness of heart," Jesus said to his contemporary antagonists, Moses "wrote you this commandment."

The statement is a poignant indictment of the human audiences. Jesus was saying that the divorce permission Moses gave was not God's perfect design but rather a concession to the human beings with which he was dealing. Like the parent who plans a special occasion for the family, but then has to adjust the plan because of the child's selfishness or misbehavior. Everything would have been lovelier if the child had simply behaved properly, but the perfect, original plan had to be scaled back because something was broken or taken away.

Yet Jesus does not pin the trouble on just the generation of people who surrounded Moses. "Because of your hardness of heart," he says. Jesus makes no distinction between Moses' audience and his own. They are all one, inasmuch as what was wrong with the one is still what is wrong with the other.

The writer of Ecclesiastes declared that there is "nothing new under the sun" (1:19). That may not be true in the details of human knowledge and technology, but it is certainly true in the realm of human behavior. We haven't invented any new sins or any new virtues. We may have some distinctive ways of acting out our sinfulness that were unknown to previous generations, but the underlying condition of a fallen humanity remains the same. The condition of Jesus' audience was just as problematic as the condition of Moses' audience. And from what I know of the human creature, I suspect that our condition is much the same as theirs.

And what is that chronic, human condition? Jesus captures it in a single word.

The Damning Diagnosis

Sklerokardia is a word we might expect to hear from a medical doctor. It's a Greek word from the New Testament, but we recognize within it syllables that are familiar to us in English. *Sclerosis* is a term we know well from a variety of medical contexts. Merriam-Webster defines it as "a disease in which soft parts inside the body become hard." And *kardia*, of course, brings to mind our words *cardio* and *cardiac*, referring to the heart.

This is the Greek word that Jesus uses to describe the condition— not medical, but spiritual condition—of the people. They suffered from *sklerokardia*. Their hearts, which are meant to be soft, had become hard.

That's a poignant condition, is it not? We know what that looks like in our human relationships, and it's always a sad sight. The bride and groom are so tenderhearted toward one another on the day they look into each other's eyes and recite their vows. But then the years pass. Perhaps, if they don't navigate those years well, the hurts, disappointments, and frustrations accumulate. And then, thirty years hence, they've become hardened toward one another—impatient, intolerant, insensitive, and unforgiving. How sad when that which is meant to be soft becomes hard!

I saw it at another level when I was in my twenties and didn't have any children of my own yet. I was working as a youth minister, while my wife was running an in-home daycare for a handful of children in our home. Every weekday, therefore, I would see parents with their babies and toddlers, and every weekend I would see parents with their teens. And I wondered what happened during those intervening years! The eyes of both the parents and their toddlers would light up when they would see each other at pickup time. They would run to each other and embrace with warmth and enthusiasm. But I did not see much of that warmth and enthusiasm between the teenagers and their parents. I saw, instead, a lot of eye-rolling and mutual frustration. I know better than to think that the change was necessarily a permanent one, but still it is a sad business when a heart that was soft turns hard.

This, according to Jesus, was the critical condition of the people of Moses' day. Moses had to make concessions to the hard-heartedness of his people. And Jesus knew that the antagonists gathered around him that day suffered from the same condition. They may have talked a good game and mimicked a sort of superficial righteousness, but something was wrong on the inside. A hardening of the heart.

God's Sand Wedge

I came late to the game of golf. I had grown up in more of a football and basketball family, but I married into a tennis and golf family. I discovered that those are quite different sports. The harshest lesson came as I learned that while frustration and anger could be useful on the football field or basketball court, they were death knells to the tennis player or the golfer.

When I joined my wife's family on their vacations, my father-in-law loaned me an old set of his golf clubs so that I could be part of a family foursome. I'm sure I was quite pathetic. But it was a good learning experience for me, and the in-laws were patient and kind.

Part of the educational process for a non-golfer was getting acquainted with the variety of clubs that comprise a golfer's bag. I had only played miniature golf; putters were all I knew. But now I was being introduced to a wealth of choices each time I considered my next shot.

I demonstrated an early attraction to water. While earlier generations employed a divining rod to find water, I'm sure I could walk into a desert with a golf club and get the job done. And I learned that there was no club in the bag to remedy the shots that landed in water.

Then I discovered sand. On my first visit to a sand trap, my father-in-law pointed out to me the sharply angled club in my bag that he called the sand wedge. "This will help you get out of the sand," he explained, and then he demonstrated how I should line it up and the sort of stroke I should use.

You don't want to be in a sand trap, of course, but given the likelihood that you will be, you want to have the right tool for the job. You want to have a wedge. Carrying that club in your bag is a concession to the unhappy reality of sand traps.

The Law of God is a like a sand wedge. Just as the golfer has to play the ball where it lies, even if it lies where the golfer doesn't want it to be, so it is with God and us. The Lord has to work with us where we are and as we are. We are not what God originally created and intended us to be. An earlier generation of theologians would say we are fallen. The old spiritual calls us "sin-sick souls."[1] And the lay philosopher with a mind for sports might say that we are in a sand trap, spiritually speaking.

The sand wedge helps the golfer play the ball when it's in an undesirable place. And the Law serves the same sort of purpose for God. The Law is how God works with where we are.

Under the Circumstances

Leslie Weatherhead was a pastor and preacher in London during World War II. As a part of his ministry in that terrible time and targeted place, he preached a brief series on the will of God. It was so wise and helpful that his pastoral messages for his own people spread far beyond that lone congregation. Still today, the slim volume containing those sermons remains in print and continues to bless people more than seventy years later.

---

1   "There Is a Balm in Gilead," *The United Methodist Hymnal*, 375.

Weatherhead famously divided the will of God into three categories. The "intentional" will of God was Weatherhead's term for the original, perfect will of God for creation and for any particular situation. We might think of that will as embodied by the garden of Eden.

At the other end of the time line, Weatherhead spoke of the "ultimate" will of God. That will is the perfection that God will eventually accomplish in the end. Biblical pictures of the peaceable kingdom (Isaiah 11:6-9) or the new heaven, new earth, and New Jerusalem (Revelation 21) might capture what we mean by that ultimate will of God.

But then there is life in this world in between. Life in the meantime. The present, imperfect reality between Paradise and the peaceable kingdom. And Weatherhead writes about God's will in the midst of the present reality as the "circumstantial" will of God.

If things were perfect, then there would be no need for medicine or surgery, no need for food pantries and homeless shelters, no need for police forces and fire departments. But things are not perfect, and therefore we embrace all of those enterprises as instruments of God's will under the circumstances. They are all sand wedges, you see.

The Old Testament Law is an expression of what Weatherhead calls the circumstantial will of God. The people of the ancient nation of Israel were not perfect, and they were not living in the midst of a perfect world. It was a world of wars, slavery, and poverty. It was a world marred by crime, broken relationships, and perversion. It was, you see, a world very much like ours. And the Law that God gave to those people was an expression of God's will in the midst of such imperfect circumstances.

This is the poignant picture painted by Jesus. God's perfect will for marriage is embodied by the story of Creation and Eden. But the Law was not given in the days of Adam and Eve, it was given in the days of Moses. It was not given to perfect people, but to people of hardened hearts. And so, "because of your hardness of heart"—under the circumstances, in the sand trap—"he wrote you this commandment."

So let us consider a few specific examples that will help us to see what God's circumstantial will looks like in the Law.

An Eye for An Eye

In the marvelous 1971 movie musical, *Fiddler on the Roof*, the lead character, Tevye, hears some friends discussing the standard in the Jewish law that says "an eye for an eye and a tooth for a tooth." He is put off by what he hears. And so he replies, sardonically, "Very good. That way the whole world will be blind and toothless."[2]

The response is charming and witty, yet I think that it reflects a fundamental misunderstanding of the Law. We hear "an eye for an eye," and we hear violence and vindictiveness. In reality, though, God established that Law in order to restrain both.

We human beings have an impulse for vengeance. When someone wrongs us, we want our pound of flesh. And we see that this instinct within us runs deep, for even very young children on the playground exhibit the tit-for-tat behavior. This one pushes, and the other pushes back. This one grabs a toy, and the other yanks it back.

We think of revenge as "getting even." In reality, of course, "even" is very rarely what people try to get. For our vengeance impulse is not informed merely by a sense of justice. Some ego gets mixed in. Some personal indignation contaminates the desire for justice. And so we seek more than just "even."

Isn't it interesting that the expression is not "tat for tat"? No, it's "tit for tat." Merriam-Webster speculates that the current idiom is a variation on an original "tip for tap." In other words, you tap me

---

2   Joseph Stein, screenplay, *Fiddler on the Roof* (United Artists, 1971).

and, in response, I endeavor to tip you over. The response is not proportionate, you see. The response is an overreaction.

In the Old Testament Law, therefore, God established this standard for penalizing offenses. "You shall appoint as a penalty life for life, eye for eye, tooth for tooth, hand for hand, foot for foot, burn for burn, wound for wound, bruise for bruise" (Exodus 21:23-25). It is "tat for tat," you see, which was designed precisely to avoid "tit for tat."

In a perfect world, you don't need such a law, such a standard. But God's Law was not being given to perfect people in a perfect world. Rather, the reality of the situation was a world where people were going to wrong one another, hurt one another, offend one another. And so the Lord built into the Law a standard for justice that was designed to keep the violence and the hurt from escalating. It was simple, dispassionate, and just: an eye for an eye. And under the circumstances, the Law was wise and good.

Cutting Corners

Those of us who have missed a turn while trying to follow the instructions of a GPS are familiar with the phrase "recalculating route." The fact that we took a wrong turn along the way doesn't mean we can no longer reach our destination. It does mean, however, that the route needs to be adjusted somewhat.

So, too, the circumstantial will of God acknowledges a departure from the best and original route, which was the intentional will of God. But that circumstantial will is the recalculated route: it becomes the path that goes from a fallen world to the ultimate will of God. And one of the course corrections we see in the Law of God is Israel's prescribed response to poverty.

Poverty is not God's will. The abundance with which God surrounded Adam and Eve in Eden gives us a glimpse of the perfect design. Likewise, it's hard to imagine that there will be any want in heaven. No starving people, desperate and begging, living homelessly on the streets of gold.

But while poverty is not God's perfect will, it is part of the reality in the meantime. Israel would have in their midst people who were poor and needy, people who lacked the ability or resources to fend for themselves, people who were for some reason marginalized. And so God's Law had built-in accommodations for those folks within Israelite society.

First, the Lord created what we might call a safety net in the regulations regarding tithing. The tithe represented the first 10 percent of a person's harvest or herds. Two out of every three years, the tithe was to be used in the worship of God. But "at the end of every third year you shall bring out all the tithe of your produce in that year, and shall deposit *it* in your town. The Levite, because he has no portion or inheritance among you, and the alien, the orphan and the widow who are in your town, shall come and eat and be satisfied, in order that the LORD your God may bless you in all the work of your hand which you do" (Deuteronomy 14:28-29).

A second part of God's designed safety net was the Year of Jubilee (see Leviticus 25). This unique holiday within Israel's calendar was scheduled for every fiftieth year. On that glorious occasion, the debts were canceled, slaves were released, and land that had been forfeited or sold along the way was returned to its original owner. In our day, we understand the phenomenon of generational poverty. But the Law built a hedge against such a development by preventing a family from losing all they had and becoming hopelessly needy.

Furthermore, the Law was deliberate about insisting on equal justice for all. Here, again, is evidence of the hard-nosed realism of God's Law. Clearly any system of human justice will have frailties built into it because human beings are frail. There's always a risk, therefore, that those with greater resources will enjoy greater "justice."

And so the Law was explicit about God's expectations: "Do not deny justice to your poor people in their lawsuits" (Exodus 23:6 NIV). The Law also protected the poor who were forced to borrow money. "If you lend money to My people, to the poor among you," the Lord said, "you are not to act as a creditor to him; you shall not charge him interest" (Exodus 22:25). Furthermore, if the poor borrower offered his cloak as collateral, God required that it be returned at night "that he may sleep in his cloak and bless you; and it will be righteousness for you before the LORD your God" (Deuteronomy 24:13). And, similarly, the wages due to a poor man were not to be withheld for even a single day. The employer was to pay him before the sun set each day, "for he is poor and sets his heart on it" (Deuteronomy 24:15).

Perhaps the most lovely law of all with regard to the poor, though, was God's command to cut corners. When the Israelites harvested their fields, the Lord instructed them not to harvest thoroughly, end to end and side to side. Rather, they were to leave the corners and edges of their fields unharvested. Likewise, they were not to gather all of the grapes from their vineyards. Rather, "you shall leave them for the needy and for the stranger" (Leviticus 19:10).

The image is a marvelous example for us in our day too. Do we harvest every square inch of our budgets? Do we consume thoroughly our contemporary harvests? Or do we leave margins so that we have something to offer the poor passerby?

We cherish the image of Lady Justice being blind, and that's fine. But God's Law was not blind. Its eyes were wide open to the reality of the fallen world—imperfect circumstances, sand traps, and hardened hearts. And so the Law matter-of-factly concedes, "the poor will never cease to be in the land." What, then, is God's response under the circumstances? "Therefore I command you, saying, 'You shall freely open your hand to your brother, to your needy and poor in your land' " (Deuteronomy 15:11).

Slaves in God's Economy

I know of a marvelous young woman from a church I served years ago. Her marriage is lovely, her children are wonderful, and her walk with God is exemplary. I also remember, however, that as a sixteen- and seventeen-year-old, she was in quite a different place. Her parents were brokenhearted over some of the choices she was making and the way she was living. There was tremendous tension and strife in their home back then as they worked to curtail her youthful folly.

Interestingly, I'm told that this young woman has reflected back on those teenage years and said to her folks that they should have been more strict with her. The mother and father look at each other and shake their heads, of course. They remember how their strictness went over back then. Whatever rules and discipline they had tried to enforce seemed to result only in fighting, resentment, and rebellion. It's all past now, and the relationships are reconciled and beautiful. But at the time, things were very rough between them and their daughter.

I am reminded of that family—and of that young woman in particular—when I hear some folks' critique of the Old Testament Law. They look back and wish that God had been more strict. Why did the Lord put up with some of the things the people did, we wonder. And I suspect the Lord shakes his head, knowing how we human beings resist and resent the divine rules and discipline.

Two particular areas where the modern reader feels some impatience with the ancient law are slavery and warfare. The Law includes all sorts of rules about the treatment of slaves, when we wish that the Law had simply outlawed slavery. Those rules, therefore, sound to us like an endorsement of the system where we want to hear a condemnation. Likewise, the Law includes rules for warfare. But something within us longs for God's Law to aim at peace—indeed, to insist on it. God should have been more strict, we think, with Israel's youthful folly.

But let us return to the analogy of the golfer. Are we such idealists that we think the golfer should not carry a sand wedge? Because we know that the ball should never go in the sand, do we want to outlaw the club designed to get the ball out of the sand?

The reality is that the golf course includes sand traps, so a sand wedge is required. And the lay of the land in the Bronze Age Near East included slavery and warfare. It came with the territory. And so God's Law mercifully established rules to guide Israel's behavior in both. Our focus just now is on the practice of slavery.

First, we should note that none of the slavery in ancient Israel resembled the atrocity of our American history. Israel was not engaged in the wholesale kidnapping of people from a faraway land to become their permanent property. And so we must be careful not to project our association with slavery onto their circumstance.

Furthermore, some of the slavery in that cultural context was actually self-inflicted. Slavery was a systemic solution for indebtedness. A person whose circumstances forced him into owing a great deal of money did not have our array of financial institutions to extend credit. A common option, therefore, was sell yourself into someone's service. It was not hyperbole when the writer of Proverbs said, "The rich rules over the poor, And the borrower becomes the lender's slave" (Proverbs 22:7).

Now, it seems that there was a practice of using conquered peoples as slave labor. Slavery was simply a part of that ancient world. Yet, within the landscape of that existing reality of slavery, the Law required certain treatment of slaves.

The slave, for example, was included in the Sabbath rest (Exodus 23:12). The master of the house didn't put his feet up on the Sabbath day while the slaves continued to labor away. No, the slaves, too, were free from all work on the Sabbath.

Even within the cultural context of slavery, the Law instructed the Israelites to give sanctuary to runaway slaves and not hand them over to their masters (Deuteronomy 23:15). Also, rules of compensation discouraged masters from treating their slaves harshly (Exodus 21:26-27). Furthermore, the Lord sought to cultivate compassion within the Israelites by reminding them of their own experience of being slaves in Egypt (for example, Deuteronomy 15:15, 16:12, 24:18).

Meanwhile, God's Law prevented slavery from being a permanent condition for the Hebrews. Even a "purchased" person was not to be regarded as permanent property, for every Hebrew slave was to be set free automatically in the seventh year (Exodus 21:2). And when the slave was set free, it was not to be done begrudgingly, but generously. "When you set him free, you shall not send him away empty-handed. You shall furnish him liberally from your flock and from your threshing floor and from your wine vat; you shall give to him as the LORD your God has blessed you" (Deuteronomy 15:13-14).

And, finally, here is a remarkable testament to the atmosphere of kindness and compassion towards slaves that God sought to create. The Law even anticipated the possibility of a slave loving his master and not wanting to go free (Exodus 21:5)! This, you see, is the sign of a great shot even when the ball is in the sand trap.

7

The Sanctities of Life

You must not yield to or heed any such persons. Show
them no pity or compassion and do not shield them.

Deuteronomy 13:8 NRSV

Some people get into a swimming pool gradually. They dip in a
toe, then up to their ankles, then their knees, and so on. They start
at the shallow end, and they move into the water an inch at a time.
Other people, however, prefer to jump right in at the deep end of the
pool.

For this chapter, I'd like for us to jump right into the deep end of
the material that we need to consider. And so, let me invite you to
read these excerpts from the Old Testament Law, all from the New
Revised Standard Version:

- "Anyone who kills a human being shall be put to death"
  (Leviticus 24:17).

- "Whoever strikes father or mother shall be put to death" (Exodus 21:15).

- "Six days shall work be done, but the seventh day is a sabbath of solemn rest, holy to the LORD; whoever does any work on the sabbath day shall be put to death" (Exodus 31:15).

- "If a man commits adultery with the wife of his neighbor, both the adulterer and the adulteress shall be put to death" (Leviticus 20:10).

- "One who blasphemes the name of the LORD shall be put to death; the whole congregation shall stone the blasphemer. Aliens as well as citizens, when they blaspheme the Name, shall be put to death" (Leviticus 24:16).

- "So you shall purge the evil from your midst. If anyone secretly entices you—even if it is your brother . . . or your own son or daughter, or the wife you embrace, or your most intimate friend—saying, 'Let us go worship other gods,' . . . Stone them to death for trying to turn you away from the LORD your God" (Deuteronomy 13:5-6, 10).

Read one after another, that is a startling medley. And it prompts us to recognize another dramatic fact that we may have missed. The Ten Commandments, which many of us were taught when we were young children, are full of capital offenses. By my count, seven of the Ten Commandments were punishable by death in the larger context of the Old Testament Law.

And so, in a book that is designed to explore that Law, we have to come face-to-face with the prominence of the death penalty. And, more specifically, in a book that endeavors to unpack the beauty and goodness of the Law, we shouldn't sidestep this feature that so many people find troubling.

Surprised by Bloodshed

My experience as a local church pastor has been that a great many people did most of their Bible learning as children. In so many churches and families, the emphasis on Christian education is relegated to the elementary years, while Christian education for adults is often less about learning the Bible than discussing life issues. Consequently, when I have led folks through a cover-to-cover reading of the Bible, they are often surprised by what they find. The Bible is full of stories, after all, that we never teach to children.

It begins on the outskirts of Eden, when Cain kills Abel. And from that moment on, the pages of the Old Testament story seem to be covered with blood. The biblical narrator dispassionately tells so many bloody and brutal stories, from Cain's murderous anger to Lamech's murderous arrogance. We're appalled by how Jacob's sons avenge Dinah's rape and how Solomon avenges Shimei's curse. From Samson to Jephthah to the Levite and his concubine, we observe a violence, a brutality, and a lawlessness that seemed to characterize that time and those people.

But in the pages of Exodus, Leviticus, and Deuteronomy, we see a great deal of bloodshedding that is not at all the product of lawlessness. On the contrary, it is the product of the Law! It's one thing for the streets to be filled with blood, but quite another for the courtroom.

I have observed all through my years of ministry a common preference among church folks for the New Testament over the Old Testament. Part of what is at stake is that people prefer what they think God is like in the New to what they think God is like in the Old. They sense a greater harshness in the God of the Old Testament. And much of that feeling of harshness traces back to the Law and the prevalence of the death penalty there.

Not only does the Law prescribe the death penalty for many more crimes than we do in our culture, it even requires the death penalty for things that we don't even regard as crimes, at all. Consider the following, again from the New Revised Standard Version:

- "Whoever curses father or mother shall be put to death" (Exodus 21:17).
- "One who blasphemes the name of the LORD shall be put to death" (Leviticus 24:16).
- "A man or a woman who is a medium or a wizard shall be put to death" (Leviticus 20:27).
- "Whoever does any work on the sabbath day shall be put to death" (Exodus 31:15).

That's a lot of death penalty! But now let's redirect the focus of our cameras just a bit. Let us turn our attention from the top of Mount Sinai, from the Law and the God who gave it, to the bottom and the people to whom it was given.

Tough Crowd

You scan the crowd, and you see face after face that has been weathered and toughened by sun and wind. You see hands that are thick, broken, calloused. You observe that the skin around their wrists and ankles is all scar tissue from the chains of bondage. And you see that their backs are full of long welts and scars from the taskmasters' whips.

These are the people to whom God gave the Law: a multitude of freshly freed slaves. Every one of them was born and raised in slavery. Every one of their parents was born and raised in slavery. And now, as they camp at the foot of Mount Sinai, they have been free for a countable number of days.

Think of it this way. They had been in slavery for more years than America has been a nation. They had been out of slavery for fewer days than most of us go between haircuts. The only governing these people have known has been their taskmasters. The only law and order they have known has been whips and chains. And it is to this group of unruly people, then, that God gives rules for living.

They are not, mind you, rules meant to confine or oppress them. Rather, they are rules to teach and protect them. They are rules to train them and to keep them free.

We read the harsh penalties prescribed in the Law, and we may suspect that the people were being frightened into obedience. But, as we explored in an earlier chapter, that's not the case, at all. For God does not introduce the Law with threats, but with a reminder of what had been done for them: "I *am* the LORD your God, who brought you out of the land of Egypt, out of the house of bondage" (Exodus 20:2 NKJV). The people's obedience to God's Law, you see, was not meant to be their fearful response to the prospect of punishment, but rather their grateful response to the God who had saved them.

In both the Old Testament and New Testament alike, punishment is not the context for obedience to God—it is salvation. The freed Hebrew slaves—and you and I—are all invited to obey not because God will punish us but because God has saved us.

That is where the Law begins, and that's where obedience begins: with salvation.

Still, the Law has a harshness to it that may trouble us. But we might understand it more clearly by observing the day-to-day relationships between parents and their children.

Parents and Children

Children, we have seen, often do not understand the passion and the forcefulness of their parents' reaction to certain things. When the child goes running toward the street or is about to put something in his or her mouth or picks up something that is valuable and fragile, the child seldom understands why Mom or Dad reacts so vigorously. As young children, they are startled by it. As older children, they are annoyed by it. But children so often do not understand what things are truly important or truly valuable or truly dangerous. And as it goes with children and their parents, so it goes with us and our God.

God's rules and penalties instruct us in matters of importance and value and danger—matters that we might not otherwise recognize or understand. When we read the penalties that God builds into the Law, therefore, let us read them as though they were "price tags," indicators of value. And that includes, especially, the frequent use of the death penalty.

Our modern society employs the death penalty only in cases where the crimes are considered especially heinous. But when we read the Old Testament Law, we see the death penalty invoked for things that do not seem heinous to us at all.

But the ethos of Scripture is different from the ethos of our culture. As the people of God, you and I are obliged to understand and observe that difference. And I would suggest that the line distinguishing our culture from God's Law is the line between the words *heinous* and *holy*.

When we call certain acts or crimes "heinous," we reveal what things are important to us, and consequently what things offend us. God, meanwhile, designates in the Law certain things as "holy." By that designation, we learn what things are important to God and, by extension, what things offend God.

When we stop to consider the capital offenses in the Old Testament, I suggest that we discover a list of things that are holy. God is holy. God's name is holy. God's day is holy. So, too, it seems are human life, parents, marriage, and sexuality. These are all holy, and we are not to be careless with holy things.

The Value of Life

The modern reader is offended by so many Old Testament stories—brutal episodes from the pages of Genesis, Judges, or Kings. We look at the events of those days, and we think that life was cheap then. However, if characters from those times and places would read our newspapers or watch our televisions, would they come to the same conclusion about us and our day?

But then the modern reader is also offended not just by the stories, but also by so many parts of the Old Testament Law. The frequent invocation of the death penalty startles us. And we conclude, again, that human life was cheap and that the Law treats human life lightly.

I suspect the truth, however, is quite the opposite. I wonder if, in reality, the Old Testament Law takes human life more seriously than we do. For the real sanctity of life is not found in merely preserving physical existence. The sanctity of life is found in preserving as sacred those things in life that are sacred.

You and I live in a culture that has largely forgotten the sanctities of life. We're very much aware of the niceties and conveniences of life, but not the sanctities. I'm afraid that we have lost our way when it comes to matters of holiness. For holiness, after all, implies a vertical measure, but we have become devoted to an exclusively horizontal measure. Legislation, morality, and ethics are almost entirely dictated now by how a word or deed affects another human being. Long forgotten, though, is any public consideration of how our words or deeds affect God.

Yet that is the very heart of the matter in the Old Testament Law. The first four of the Ten Commandments set the standard, for they are instructions that have no direct impact on any other human being: they are simply matters of proper reverence for God. And as we unpack the "horizontal" commands in the Law—how we treat other people—we discover that the underpinning for those is also the holiness of God. In that sense, how the Israelites were taught to treat other people was really, at its core, more a response to the Lord than to those people.

We see this principle percolating through the rest of Scripture as well. The writer of Proverbs, for example, draws the line connecting the poor and God. "One who is gracious to a poor man lends to the LORD, And He will repay him for his good deed" (19:17). And that, in turn, reminds us of Jesus' story of the sheep and the goats (Matthew 25:31-46). The crucial issue, we discover, is not merely how we treat the hungry, the thirsty, and the sick, but how we are thus treating the Lord.

The most dramatic expression of this principle, meanwhile, is found in Jesus' "new commandment." At the Last Supper, Jesus tells his followers, "A new command I give you: Love one another. As I have loved you, so you must love one another" (John 13:34 NIV). Our love for each another, you see, is not meant simply to be a response to each other. No, our human love is a response to Divine love. Our horizontal relationships are an extension and response to the vertical relationship—our relationship with God.

The Old Testament Law reminds us of a truth that our surrounding culture has forgotten. We live our lives before a holy God, and how we live is meant to be a conscious response to that holiness. You and I are called, therefore, to be attentive to the sanctities of life.

God's People Then and Now

We see those weathered faces and tough souls gathered around Mount Sinai to receive God's Law. How much do we feel we have in common with them? They lived in such a different time and different place. Their circumstances seem so far removed from ours. Yet we worship the same God, and we are recipients of the same Law.

Perhaps we are not as different as we think. Still today, after all, God's people are a group of freed slaves, for Paul says that we were slaves to sin and Christ has set us free (Romans 6). Still today, God's rules instruct us in what is important, what is valuable, what is dangerous. And still today, our obedience need not spring out of fear of being punished but rather out of gratitude for being saved.

And then there is this other matter that rises above any particularities of time or place. Both we and the ancient Israelites have the same calling. So even if we come from different places, our destination is the same. And that destination is holiness.

We noted earlier the Lord's expressed will that we should be like him. It is revealed in the Creation story, and it is repeated in the instructions of the Law, the expectations of the prophets, the teachings of Jesus, and the exhortations of the apostles. And central to becoming like God is being a holy people. "Speak to all the congregation of the sons of Israel," the Lord instructed Moses, "and say to them, 'You shall be holy, for I the LORD your God am holy'" (Leviticus 19:2).

When we get to the New Testament, the language of the Apostle Paul gives us an interesting insight into this high calling. He begins his letter to the Ephesians with this greeting: "Paul, an apostle of Christ Jesus by the will of God, to the saints who are at Ephesus, and who are faithful in Christ Jesus" (Ephesians 1:1). He calls his audience "saints"—a term he also uses freely in writing to the Romans, Corinthians, Philippians, and Colossians. It does not seem to be an exclusive term for unusually righteous and accomplished men and women of God. Rather, Paul employs it generously as a standard term for believers. I expect it would be the term he would use for you and me.

The interesting thing about that word as he addresses the believers in Ephesus is that, in the original Greek, it's not a noun. It reads that way in our English translations, but Paul actually used an adjective. He took an adjective, made it plural, and stuck a definite article in front of it.

Imagine that I am writing to a group of exceptionally attractive people. If I followed Paul's pattern, I would take the adjective "beautiful," make it plural, and put the definite article in front of it. I would address what I am writing to "the beautifuls."

This is what Paul has done with the word that we translate "saints." In his original Greek, he has taken the adjective "holy" and turned it into a salutation. He is calling the Christians in Ephesus "the holies."

This was the high calling of the people to whom God gave the Law three thousand years ago, and it remains our calling today. Indeed, Paul would say it is not just our calling but our identity. You and I are "holies." That doesn't assume, by the way, that we are especially good. Only that we have been chosen by and belong to the holy God.

We began this chapter with a startling collection of instructions from the Old Testament Law that employed the death penalty for all sorts of offenses. My endeavor is not to be an apologist for the death penalty, and I would not misspend your time by editorializing on what our contemporary society ought to do in matters of crime and punishment. Frankly, my purpose is much higher than that. My endeavor is to be an advocate for holiness.

Eugene Peterson, is his introduction to the book of Leviticus, calls it "a kind of extended time-out of instruction, a detailed and meticulous preparation for living 'holy' in a culture that doesn't have the faintest idea what 'holy' is."[1] I'm sure he is right. And so my goal here is to remind us that our chief concern as the people of God is not what offends or pleases us. Neither should it be what offends or pleases the culture in which we live. Rather, our chief concern must always be what offends and what pleases God: the Lord our God, who is holy, who saved us, and who continues to lead us out of the house of bondage.

---

1   Eugene Peterson, *The Message: The Old Testament Books of Moses in Contemporary Language* (Colorado Springs: NavPress, 2001), 166.

8
The Anatomy of Worship

"The priest shall then take some of the blood of the guilt
offering, and the priest shall put it on the lobe of the right
ear of the one to be cleansed, and on the thumb of his
right hand, and on the big toe of his right foot."

Leviticus 14:14

Wherever I have served in my thirty-some years of ministry, it
has always been a priority for me to help people read, study, learn,
and live the Bible as God's written word to us. And, in every place
I've served, I've challenged and encouraged people to read the whole
Bible through, start to finish, and I've developed a variety of resources
to help them do it. So it has been my great privilege over the years
to have led hundreds of people through a cover-to-cover reading of
God's word.

Over that long accumulation of experience of reading the Bible
with people, a number of recurring themes have emerged. And one

of those is a certain weariness people feel when reading all of the detailed descriptions found in the second half of Exodus and much of Leviticus. Chapter after chapter is devoted to the components and dimensions of the Tabernacle and its furnishings. Folks are also quickly satiated with information about the priests and the offerings. Altogether, the material becomes a blur of curtains and cubits, ephods and rituals, kidneys, entrails, fat, and blood.

As we read, we sometimes wonder why the Bible bothers to include all this material. And, closer to home, we wonder why we should bother to read all this material. What, after all, does it have to do with you, me, and our relationship with God?

A Lack of Curiosity

In the classic 1965 movie *The Sound of Music*, we follow the story of Captain von Trapp and his family during the time of the Nazi Anschluss of 1930s Austria. At one tense juncture near the climax of the story, the von Trapp family is endeavoring to escape from the country without the Nazi officials' knowledge. As the family members quietly push their car down the road at night, suddenly headlights illuminate them from behind, and they find themselves face-to-face with Nazi soldiers. There are a few moments of awkward conversation. Then the Nazi officer says to Captain von Trapp, "I've not asked you where you and your family are going. Nor have you asked me why I am here." And von Trapp playfully replies, "Apparently we're both suffering from a deplorable lack of curiosity."[1]

I wouldn't want to use the word deplorable. I do wonder, though, whether many of us suffer from at least a regrettable lack of curiosity when it comes to this material in the Law. Or perhaps a still better word would be ironic. We suffer from an ironic lack of curiosity.

---

1   Ernest Lehman, screenplay, *The Sound of Music* (Twentieth Century Fox, 1965).

So many times in my years of Bible teaching, folks have asked me a question about some character or event, and I have had to say that I don't know the answer because the Bible doesn't give us the answer. The Bible doesn't tell us what Jesus looked like. It doesn't explain what Paul's thorn in the flesh was. It doesn't record for us what happened to most of the disciples. It doesn't reveal where the ark of the covenant ended up. There are lots of things we become curious about as we read, but the Bible doesn't satisfy our curiosity on those points.

In the case of the Tabernacle and the worship life of the early Israelites, however, the Bible does give us the details. We are not left to wonder what it all looked like, what the priests and the people did, or what instructions God gave them. We don't have to wonder because we have that material. We know the sizes, the colors, the shapes, and the designs. At some level, therefore, we really ought to be thankful for these chapters and all of their details.

Children and teenagers in school are often taught information about things before they are actually curious about them, so they think the material is boring. In fact, the material is not at all boring—they just aren't interested in it yet. Chances are that, some years later, they will have the basis to be interested, and then they will look back and wish that they had listened more carefully to what they were being taught about that period of history, that part of science, those pieces of literature, and such.

You and I, meanwhile, are mature enough to recognize that if we did not have the information contained in Exodus and Leviticus, we would probably be curious to know what it was all like. And so for that reason, even though we complain about them, these details are precious to us.

Acts of Worship

Still, there is something bigger involved. The details of the Tabernacle, the sacrifices, the holy days, and such are important to us not only because they satisfy some detached, historical curiosity on our part. The details of Exodus and Leviticus are precious to us because they reflect how the Lord instructed the people Israel to worship.

We see, then, how this is much more than a mere matter of curiosity. This is of supreme contemporary relevance to us. If we are dealing with the same God, then we have a treasure buried in these chapters, for they contain an expression of how we are to worship.

Again, we recall the "speed limit" analogy. The idea is not that we go exactly the same speed as the ancient Israelites did—that we worship precisely the same way. The idea, rather, is that we recognize the underlying and guiding principles that God built into their worship. And one of those principles—perhaps a surprising one for some of us—is that worship is a physical act.

The parts of the Law that explicate the worship life of Israel are chock-full of physical details. Bringing and lifting, cutting and burning, sprinkling and pouring, washing and draining. And the physical details that are given prompt us to imagine still more. We can feel the heat radiating off the fire on the altar. We can smell the rich mixture of fragrances—live animals, burning incense, and smoking sacrifices. We envision the colors of the Tabernacle and the priestly regalia. We imagine the sounds of bleating and mooing, crackling fire, and the voices of worshipers.

My contention in all of this is not that our worship services should mimic the rituals of ancient Israel. I do believe, though, that woven through those rituals are principles for us to apply and truths for us to understand. And that includes the very physical-ness of their worship.

In the next chapter, we will turn our attention to the physical place of worship carefully detailed in the Law. For now, though, we want to give some thought to the physical acts of worship prescribed for the Israelites. And the first great key is to recognize that they are truly physical acts.

It is not uncommon these days to hear someone say that they aren't "religious" but that they are very "spiritual." That means different things to different people, of course, but they are right in what they say, for they are spiritual. All human beings are spiritual. It is part of how God created us.

When the Book of Genesis describes the creation of humankind, it is remarkably simple and succinct: "The LORD God formed man of dust from the ground, and breathed into his nostrils the breath of life; and man became a living being" (2:7). Two elements, you see. Two ingredients: dust from the ground and breath from God. The Hebrew word for *breath* is also the word for *spirit*. And so Genesis reveals that we human beings are a mysterious marriage of physical and spiritual. It is the same two-part composition that Jesus himself references in Gethsemane when he says of his disciples, "The spirit is willing, but the flesh is weak" (Mark 14:38).

Spirit and flesh. You are both. I am both. And those two parts are not separated like oil and water, but rather they are magnificently mixed and mysteriously intertwined so that you can hardly find the border between them and so that each affects the other. Our spirits impact our bodies, and our bodies affect our spirits.

Of Hips and Knees

In February 1996, my dad took a fall while walking across a slippery sidewalk, and he broke his hip. He was two days shy of seventy-three at the time. He needed to have hip replacement surgery, and then he went through the rehab process following the surgery. And when it was all done, he discovered that he had lost three things.

First, he lost some speed: he was not able to walk as briskly as he had before. Second, he lost some enjoyment. Walking had always been a real source of pleasure for my dad, but now there was just enough discomfort and added caution that walking was not as enjoyable as it had always been for him before. And, third, he lost some of his ability to kneel.

His custom every morning for decades had been to spend time kneeling in prayer. I can still picture from my childhood the living room chair where he would kneel to pray each morning.

With the hip replacement, however, he found that he needed to be able to brace himself more in order to get back up off of his knees, and he didn't really have a chair that suited the purpose. And so, he resigned himself to sitting when he prayed each morning.

Then, perhaps a dozen or so years later, he was given a very handsome chair as a gift, and he was delighted to discover that the design and structure of that chair was such that he could kneel in front of it and still be able to get back to his feet.

Shortly after receiving that gift, he wrote: "Since then I've begun my morning time with God each day kneeling at this chair. . . . I don't think the posture matters to God, but it matters to me. I need, at the beginning of each day, to get on my knees, put my face in my hands . . . and remind myself that God is God and I am not."[2]

C. S. Lewis made a similar sort of point in his creative and insightful little book, *The Screwtape Letters*. The book pretends to be a series of letters written by a senior demon to a junior demon, offering counsel and instruction about how to keep a person from God. And along the way, the senior demon offers this insight about human beings: "They can be persuaded that the bodily position makes no difference to their prayers; for they constantly forget . . . that they are animals and that whatever their bodies do affects their souls."[3]

This was my dad's conclusion about kneeling: that while his posture didn't necessarily matter to God, it mattered to him because it affected him. His posture affected him. His body affected his soul.

---

2   J. Ellsworth Kalas, "The Right Posture," Asbury Theological Seminary *Alumni Link*, https://asburyseminary.edu/elink/the-right-posture/, accessed November 21, 2018.

3   C. S. Lewis, *The Screwtape Letters* (San Francisco: HarperCollins, 1996), 16.

Meeting Us Where We Are

We read the abundance of physical details in the Old Testament Law regarding Israel's worship life, and we think it a bit tedious. But perhaps those physical details are part of how God meets us where we are. Perhaps the Law is inescapably physical because you and I are inescapably physical.

We noted earlier the Genesis account of God creating human beings. The man is not a living being just because the physical form is crafted. God must breathe into that physique the breath of life—spirit into flesh—and then "man became a living being." And I believe that since that is the pattern for how God created us in the first place, it remains the pattern for how God continues to deal with us.

Consider the sprinkling with blood, the anointing with oil, and the circumcision of the flesh that we see in the Old Testament. Does the first really purify a thing? Does the second actually equip a person for priestly service? Is the third truly essential for a relationship with the Lord? Yet these are all instruments of God in the Law.

One recent Sunday morning, our Sunday custodian had forgotten to put water in our baptismal font, and I was scheduled to baptize a child that day. As the service was about to start, I realized that there was no water in the font, and so I asked the woman who was assisting me in worship leadership that day to fill the bowl with water for us while I began leading the service. She wondered where she should get the water. And I think she was a bit surprised to learn that she should get it from the faucet in the church kitchen.

The water comes from the faucet. The bread and juice come from the grocery store. The makings of our sacraments are common and ordinary elements. But that shouldn't surprise us, for God chose the most common and un-extraordinary thing of all in order to make us in the first place: dust. Ah, but when the Spirit fills that dust, then it comes alive!

So, too, I believe God's Spirit brings sacredness and life to all sorts of ordinary, physical things. By itself, the olive oil is ineffectual. By itself, the circumcision is merely a medical procedure. By itself, the sprinkled blood will only leave stains. But the Spirit flows through physical acts and fills physical vessels in order to accomplish God's purpose in us.

Our worship of God is necessarily both physical and spiritual, you see. Not for God's sake, but for ours. In the worship guidelines of the Law, the Lord meets us where we are, for you and I are both physical and spiritual.

No Body Shaming in Scripture

"I believe in God the Father Almighty, maker of heaven and earth." This is our first declaration in the Apostles' Creed, our most fundamental expression of what we believe. And while, in our scientific age, "maker" has become the controversial claim, for so many earlier generations the radical word was *earth*. The debate was over God's relation to the material world.

The Gnostics were perhaps the most famous ones to deny God's involvement in creating the physical world. It's not that they didn't believe in God. Rather, they stand as part of a long line of folks throughout history who have doubted that a good, holy, and spiritual God could be responsible for this fallen, corruptible, material world. They conceded the basic spirit-and-flesh paradigm of our existence, but they denied the unity of those elements. Rather, the one was regarded as higher and good, while the other was lower and bad. Spiritual things were of God. Material things, however, were the result of some inferior, perhaps even malevolent being.

When the earliest centuries of Christians affirmed that God was "maker of heaven and earth," therefore, they were stubbornly asserting the testimony of Scripture over the popular philosophies and "enlightened" thinking of their day. And the unrelenting testimony of Scripture is that God is responsible for and invested in this physical world. We affirm it at the beginning of the Apostles' Creed when we call God "maker of . . . earth." We affirm it again when we say that Jesus was "born of the Virgin Mary." And we affirm it yet again when we declare that we believe in "the resurrection of the body." From creation to incarnation to resurrection, the Bible consistently affirms the Lord's positive relationship with the physical, material world. Indeed, the final picture painted for us in Scripture is not merely of a new heaven, but a new heaven and a new earth (Revelation 21:1).

Still today, so many folks try to bifurcate human experience, separating the physical parts of human life from the spiritual parts. The person who says that he or she is a "spiritual person," therefore, is right, but only half right. They are a "spiritual person," to be sure, but they are a "physical person," too. Such is the way that God made us. And we cut across the grain of God's design when we try to separate the two.

In our relationship with God, therefore, we must be careful not to parcel off things like prayer and worship as though they are exclusively spiritual. They are not because we are not. And such segregating of the things of God to a spiritual-only mentality not only shortchanges our experience of those things but also risks that we will not fully integrate God into the physical parts of our lives.

So it is that the worship instructions from God in the Old Testament Law are irrepressibly physical instructions and full of physical details. The dimensions and the designs, the colors and the fragrances, the detailed anatomy of it all is God speaking our language. We are creatures of time and space, and so our worship of God takes time and takes place.

Rather than seeming distant and foreign, therefore, I believe this material should actually seem beautifully familiar to us. When we are baptized in water, we bear witness that we are both physical and spiritual creatures. When we partake of the bread and the cup as a means of grace, we bear witness that spirit and flesh are intertwined. And when we set aside a time to fast and pray, we bear witness that our life in Christ is two-part.

And our life in the world is meant to be two-part as well. Not only does the physical enter into our worship of God, but our worship of God must enter into the physical. So it is that the Apostle Paul writes to the Christians in Corinth, saying, "Do you not know that your body is a temple of the Holy Spirit . . . and that you are not your own? For you have been bought with a price: therefore glorify God in your body" (1 Corinthians 6:19-20).

The whole integrated truth finds its fullest expression in Paul's exhortation to the Christians in Rome. "I appeal to you therefore, brothers and sisters," he writes, "by the mercies of God, to present your bodies as a living sacrifice, holy and acceptable to God, which is your spiritual worship" (Romans 12:1 NRSV).

Against the backdrop of the Old Testament altar and its sacrificial worship, Paul's image of presenting our bodies as living sacrifices has real meaning for us. We remember that to offer something to God was the essential act of worship. We recall, too, that the people were not to bring to the Lord half-hearted leftovers, but their first and their best. And we are struck by the sudden holiness of a sacrifice. What was an ordinary sheep or goat thirty minutes earlier is now a sacred thing—not because of any merit of its own, but because it has been dedicated to God. And what has been dedicated to God at the altar cannot be retracted. It belongs to the Lord.

Finally, in his provocative exhortation to the Romans, the apostle suggests a fascinating principle: that our "spiritual worship" is to offer our bodies. No segregating of spirit and flesh here. From the creation of Adam until the present moment, those two elements have been knit together within us. Naturally, therefore, they belong together in our worship. And what God taught the Israelites in their Law, you and I must also bear in mind—that our spirit and flesh go together in our living relationship with the One who created us in the first place, who put on our flesh to redeem us, and who promises to raise us up on the last day.

The stuff of Exodus and Leviticus, you see, is not an Old Testament idiosyncrasy. It is a thoroughly human beauty. And, from beginning to end, it is God's design.

9
Tour the Tabernacle

"Make this tabernacle and all its furnishings exactly like the pattern I will show you."

Exodus 25:9 NIV

One Christmas break when I was a teenager, my older sister came home from college and sang to us a song that she had written. Well, she didn't so much sing it to us as we heard her singing it around the house off and on all through that week. It was thirteen verses long. It was called, "I Hate French."

Evidently she was not happy with the French class and French professor that she had that semester, so she put her frustration to music.

That was more than forty years ago. Today, my sister is a tenured professor in French language and literature. So clearly something happened—some positive thing happened—since that Christmas break. Some other professor or two must have come along and helped her to fall in love with material that once had her feeling fed up.

Perhaps some of us have a similar story in some area of life. Perhaps for you there is a subject, a sport, a hobby, a kind of music, or some such that you once disliked, but then someone came along and made all the difference for you in that area. That is the sort of experience I would like for us to have in this chapter. Imagine some museum or historic site that you have visited before, but without much enjoyment or appreciation. You didn't get much out of it the first time you went there.

Then the writer of the New Testament letter to the Hebrews comes along, and he offers to be our tour guide. He wants us to revisit that same historic site, that same museum, but now to do it with him. He intends for us to hear about it from him, to see it through his eyes. And the result will be that, what once was dry as dust and irrelevant, will become deeply meaningful to us.

Now in reality, the writer of Hebrews is our main guide, but he is not our only guide. The Apostle Paul will also help, as will the Gospel writers. And the old, uninteresting place that they want to lead us back through once more is the Tabernacle.

The Tabernacle from Above

The Tabernacle, you recall, was the portable place of worship that Moses and the people of Israel constructed according to God's design. It was a portable place of worship because it was designed for their use during their nomadic years: the period of traveling through the wilderness between Egypt and the Promised Land. Three of the twelve tribes of Israel camped together toward the east, three together toward the west, three more to the north, and the remaining three to the south. And the Tabernacle compound was set up right in the middle of it all.

While the children of Israel were living in tents, the Tabernacle was understood to be God's tent. It was the Lord's dwelling place, the place of God's presence and glory. And, by God's design, it was right in the middle of the camp, central in the midst of God's people.

God did not choose to live at a distance from the people. The Lord was not sequestered at the holy mountain of Sinai. Neither was God waiting for the people finally to catch up in Canaan. God was not removed from them by some safe distance. On the contrary, the Lord dwelt in their midst.

The Old Testament Hebrew word that we translate as *Tabernacle* meant "dwelling place." And, likewise, the New Testament Greek verb that we translate as *dwell* meant "to have one's tabernacle." Accordingly, when the Gospel of John tells us of the incarnation of Christ, it says this: "The Word was made flesh, and dwelt among us, (and we beheld his glory, the glory as of the only begotten of the Father,) full of grace and truth" (John 1:14 KJV).

The Word became flesh and dwelt among us. *Dwelt*—the underlying Greek word is the one that meant "to have one's tabernacle." The Gospel is saying, you see, that Christ put on flesh and made his tabernacle in our midst.

So let us imagine that our tour of the Tabernacle begins with a bird's-eye view of ancient Israel's campsite in the wilderness. From high in the air, we see God's Tabernacle right in the midst of the people. And from above, we observe that the Tabernacle featured a spacious, open-air courtyard, as well as a large, colorful tent within that courtyard. That Tent, then, was God's dwelling place. The open-air courtyard was in a rectangular shape, and it was partitioned off by tall, portable dividers. Even though the Israelites were camped on all sides of the Tabernacle, it did not have entrances on all sides. There was just one entrance, just one way to access that place where God dwelled.

During the Last Supper, Thomas asked Jesus to show him and the other disciples the way to the Father. Jesus replied, "I am the way, and the truth, and the life; no one comes to the Father, but through Me" (John 14:6).

Altar Call

Having seen the Tabernacle compound from above, our tour takes us next to ground level. Now, we can experience it the way those ancient Israelite worshipers did. We work our way around to the side that has the entrance, and we go in together.

As soon as we're within the "walls" of the Tabernacle, the first thing that meets our eyes is the great, bronze altar. One or several priests are standing nearby, attending to it. The altar was where the worshiper brought his or her sacrifices and offerings to God.

I don't know what your weekly worship service looks like, but let me ask you to imagine changing it up a bit. First, is music a part of your service? Let's pretend that we take out all of the music. No choir, no band, no organ, no congregational singing—no music. Next, let's remove all teaching and preaching from the order of service. Also, no announcements, no Scripture readings, and no pastoral prayer. Certainly no children's moment. My hope is that you have a picture in your mind of a worship service that has been trimmed down to just a single component: the offering.

Imagine a church in your town redefining worship services that way. It would be a bold move, to be sure, but who would attend? Imagine inviting a friend to attend such a worship service with you.

The offering was the essential act of worship in the Old Testament Law. It's not that Israel didn't value music in its praise or instruction in its assemblies. We know better. But the centerpiece of worship in the Tabernacle was neither the organ nor the pulpit. It was the altar.

The altar was the place of human transactions with God. It was natural and right, therefore, for a later generation of evangelists to extend "altar calls." Inasmuch as the altar is the place where we offer things to God, it was the perfect place for responsive souls to offer themselves as well.

In the case of ancient Israel's worship at the altar, the book of Leviticus spells out the various kinds of offerings and the requirements for each. We read many details, and through it all, we meet with a few recurring themes.

First, we observe the emphasis on bringing to God "the first" and "the best." God's altar was no place for leftovers, for afterthoughts. Rather, this is where you brought the first fruits of your crop and the firstborn of your flocks and herds. Furthermore, if you were making an animal sacrifice, it was to be an animal "without blemish."

We read these instructions, and we are reminded of the "speed limit" principle, as you and I are challenged to offer God our first and our best in whatever we do. And, too, we remember again Paul's remarkable exhortation to the Christians in Rome. He borrows from the potent imagery of sacrifices offered on the altar, and urges those believers, saying, "I urge you therefore, brethren, by the mercies of God, to present your bodies a living and holy sacrifice, acceptable to God, which is your spiritual service of worship" (Romans 12:1). We make our very selves an offering to God.

Meanwhile, the whole system of sacrifices and offerings there at the altar was always facilitated by a priest. The priest, you see, served as the go-between—the consecrated person who was the middleman between the people and God. At any given time, there were many priests, and any one of them might have assisted you when you brought a gift to the altar. But there was only one High Priest at a time, and the High Priest served a function that no other priest could.

Into the Tent

Next, our tour takes us past the altar and toward the Tent itself. For the average Israelite worshiper, the altar was the ultimate destination—he or she went no further. But the priests had functions and responsibilities beyond the altar.

Between the altar and the Tent, we see a great bronze basin filled with water. Coming from our background, you and I might be reminded of the baptismal font or tank located prominently within our worship spaces, and that wouldn't be a bad association. The water in this basin was available for the priests to wash themselves before conducting their sacred business either at the altar or within the Tent.

Once inside the Tent, we observe that we have entered precious territory. The altar and the basin that we saw in the Tabernacle courtyard were made of or covered with bronze, but everything within the Tent is gold.

To our left, we see a tall, heavy, golden lampstand. It is highly ornate, and it is the only physical source of light inside the Holy Place. The one stand features seven lamps, reminiscent of the completeness and perfection that is represented again and again in Scripture by the number seven. The priests are responsible for maintaining the lamps on the lampstand. This is a twice-daily task for the priests, morning and evening.

To our right, we see a long table covered with gold. The express purpose of the table is to hold loaves of bread. There are twelve loaves, recalling the twelve tribes of Israel, and the priests are responsible each Sabbath for placing fresh loaves on the table. This bread is provocatively called "the bread of the Presence" (Exodus 25:30).

The instructions for the table also call for gold dishes, pans, jars, and bowls. Few details are given about the exact use of these items, apart from one brief purpose clause: "to pour drink offerings" (Exodus 25:29). The liquid to be used is not stipulated here, but elsewhere in the Law, wine is used for the drink offerings.

You and I are many years removed from that ancient Tabernacle and many miles from that wilderness. And yet we see within this Holy Place a marvelously familiar sight: a table in the place of worship, featuring bread and wine. And the bread is associated with God's presence.

The lampstand is to our left and the table to our right. Meanwhile, as we look straight ahead, we see two things. Dominating our field of vision is a curtain—floor to ceiling and wall to wall—which separates the Holy Place from the Most Holy Place. And just in front of that curtain is a small golden altar at which the priest burns incense.

The curtain—sometimes referred to as the veil—is colorful and ornate, as befitting its sacred role. The curtain represents the boundary between the Holy Place and the Most Holy Place. On the other side was only one physical item: the ark of the covenant. Its lid was known as the mercy seat. Above it, Israel understood, was the presence of God. And so the curtain was a sort of closed door between the people and God.

As we have noted, every day priests would enter the Holy Place to attend to matters there. But only the High Priest would go behind the curtain and enter the Most Holy Place, and he only did so once a year. The holiest holy day of the year for the Old Testament people of God was the Day of Atonement—what is, in our day, called Yom Kippur. On that day, the High Priest would carry the blood of a bull, which had been sacrificed as a sin offering, into the Most Holy Place. And he would sprinkle the blood from that sin offering on the mercy seat.

Meanwhile, in the New Testament, the writer of Hebrews says that Christ is our great High Priest. But he is superior to Aaron, or any of the subsequent High Priests, for he is not finite, serving only for a period of years. Rather, he lives forever. Furthermore, he is not faulty, needing to make atonement for himself and his own sins. And the writer of Hebrews notes that Christ truly enters into—comes from and returns to—the very presence of God.

Christ is our great High Priest. He has put on our flesh, walked in our shoes, known our temptations and our weaknesses. Yet he is also able to save in a way that Aaron and his descendants never could, for they themselves needed saving.

Moreover, Hebrews says that Christ himself is our atoning sacrifice. The blood of bulls and goats had to be offered again and again, year after year, generation after generation. But Christ is the perfect sacrifice: unblemished and eternal. Christ's sacrifice is once and for all.

And then there is the veil: the curtain that separated off the Most Holy Place. When the Gospels tell us about Good Friday—the day Christ died on the cross—three of them include this fascinating detail: just after he died, the curtain in the temple was torn in two. And both Matthew and Mark specifically report that it was torn from top to bottom, as if to indicate that it is God, not humans, who took the initiative to open what had been closed.

Hebrews says, "We have confidence to enter the Most Holy Place by the blood of Jesus, by a new and living way opened for us through the curtain, that is, His body" (Hebrews 10:19). And so Charles Wesley sang, "The veil is rent; in Christ alone the living way to heaven is seen; the middle wall is broken down, and all the world may enter in."[1]

The Conclusion of the Tour

Once our tour of the Tabernacle is over, we step back and see it again from a distance. We see the Tabernacle as a whole. And now we see that it is Jesus.

In C. S. Lewis' allegorical novel, *The Pilgrim's Regress*, the reader follows the journey of a pilgrim named John. Among his many encounters, he has an illuminating conversation with a hermit named History. And History explains how "the Landlord," who represents God in the allegory, has communicated with his tenants.

Those who know and understand more, History explains, "know perfectly well that the Landlord has circulated other things besides

---

1   Charles Wesley, "'Tis Finished! The Messiah Dies," *The United Methodist Hymnal*, 282.

the Rules. What use are Rules to people who cannot read? No one is born able to read: so that the starting point for all of us must be a picture and not the Rules."[2]

In Lewis's scheme, I think the distinction between pictures and Rules is what theologians classify as general revelation and special revelation. The former is that which can be known about God by all peoples in all places at all times. The latter, meanwhile, refers to the specific self-revelation of God as contained in the Scriptures of the Old and New testaments. But I think that Lewis's notion can be applied to the Old Testament Law as well. For the Law contains both rules and pictures. The rules are obvious enough—all the written commandments, instructions, and regulations. The pictures, meanwhile, may elude us. The Law gives us abundant detail so that we can see the pictures clearly. And as we see more clearly so many of the pictures in the Law, we see that they form a collage of Christ. And that begins with the Tabernacle.

Jesus is God dwelling in our midst: not God at a distance, but God with us. Jesus is the single entryway by which men and women are able to come to God. Jesus is the unblemished offering—perfect and eternally sufficient. Jesus is the great High Priest that comes between a sinful humankind and a holy God, bringing us together and making atonement for us. Jesus is the light in a dark world and the One whose presence is revealed to us in the bread and wine. Jesus is the curtain, and Jesus' death opens the way to the Father. And it is Jesus' blood that is sprinkled to make atonement, once and for all.

Perhaps upon our first reading of Exodus and Leviticus, we found the material dry and irrelevant. The writers of the New Testament, however, take us back through that same material and there help us to discover the gospel. It is *The Gospel According to Leviticus*—according to Moses, according to the sacrifices, and according to the Tabernacle.

---

2   C. S. Lewis, *The Pilgrim's Regress* (Grand Rapids: Eerdmans, 1981), 172.

An old story tells of a preacher sitting on the floor of the chancel area, surrounded by little ones, and leading the children's sermon. He began by asking them, "What is brown, has a fluffy tail, and collects nuts for the winter?" And one boy, who was a veteran of children's sermons, raised his hand and said, "The answer is probably Jesus, but it sure sounds like a squirrel to me."

The boy knew from experience that the children's sermon was likely to be, in one way or another, about Jesus. That's as it should be, of course. And we might do well to read the Bible with the same, standing expectation. Whether New Testament or Old, whether apostle or prophet, whether Gospel or Law, we may be confident that the written word of God bears witness to the incarnate Word of God.

10
A Scheduled Luxury

"You shall work six days, but on the seventh day you shall rest; even during plowing time and harvest you shall rest."

Exodus 34:21

I believe that the Fourth Commandment—the Sabbath commandment—is an imperative for our day. It is the longest of the Ten, and it is one of only two that begins with a positive command.

Eight of the Ten Commandments, you see, are worded as negative instructions. They are prohibitions. They are commandments about what not to do—make graven images, kill, commit adultery, covet, and such. Of the two positive commands, one is a command to honor, the other a command to remember.

Some people fault the Old Testament Law for seeming so negative. All of the "don't do this and don't do that" instructions seem to them rather unpleasant—hovering, controlling, persnickety. The reality is, however, that we human beings actually handle negative instructions better than we do positive ones. The negative commands represent a kind of introductory-level obedience, for it is much easier to fulfill a proscriptive command than a prescriptive one. I could, after all, spend the whole day in bed and not kill or steal. But I have to get out of bed and live a much more demanding day in order to love my neighbor as I love myself.

The two so-called positive instructions in the Ten Commandments, therefore, are the truly demanding ones. In our present culture, we struggle with both of them—both the command to remember the Sabbath and the command to honor our parents. And just now, we turn our attention to the original holy day: the Sabbath.

How Soon We Forget

The imperative used in the Fourth Commandment is ironic—or prescient. "Remember," says the Lord. Yet that is precisely what we have not done. For we have largely forgotten the Sabbath.

We might illustrate the fact by considering how Sundays have changed in America. Technically, of course, Sunday is not the Sabbath of the Old Testament Law, for it is the first day of the week rather than the seventh. Over the course of church history, however, Sundays evolved as the Christian Sabbath, as the celebration of Christ's resurrection was blended with the Old Testament observance of a weekly holy day.

Folks of a certain age will remember when Sundays in America were quite different than they are today. Stores were closed. People didn't work or shop. Most of them didn't even use Sundays for around-the-house things like cleaning or yard work. And schools didn't schedule sporting events or practices on Sundays.

Now, however, Sundays are nearly indistinguishable from any other day. Indeed, if anything, Sundays have become more crammed with commerce and activity precisely because people are generally more available on Sundays than many other days.

So what changed in, say, the past fifty or sixty years? The Bible did not change. The commandments of God did not change. No, the culture around us changed, and we mostly changed right along with it. And so the notion of the Sabbath has been gradually left behind.

The irony is that we haven't actually rejected the Sabbath. The problem is more pernicious, for it is less conscious. We've forgotten the Sabbath. We have forgotten the very thing we were commanded to remember.

In the days of King Josiah, during some repair work that was being done in the temple, a book was discovered and brought to the king's attention. The biblical narrator identifies it as "the book of the law," and when it was read to Josiah, he tore his clothes in dismay (2 Kings 22:11). Apparently the book was previously unknown to the king. Even though, generations earlier, Moses had specifically instructed that each future king of Israel should make for himself a copy of the law (Deuteronomy 17:18), it was all new to King Josiah.

Somewhere along the way, it seems, the book of the Law had gotten lost. Somehow, over the years between Moses and Josiah, God's Law had been forgotten. And so, too, in our day with God's Sabbath.

An Imaginary Poll

Let us imagine ourselves conducting a person-in-the-pew poll. We want to ask one hundred, average American churchgoers about the Ten Commandments. The question for each commandment would be, in effect, "Do you still think this is an expectation from God?"

For example, we would ask our sample focus group, "Do you still think it is an expectation from God that you not make graven images?" "Do you still think it is an expectation from God that you not steal?" "Do you still think it is an expectation from God that you honor your father and mother?"

I have never conducted such a poll. I have served in local church ministry for thirty-five years, though, and have gotten some sense for the prevailing attitudes. And so, while I don't know what the percentages would be for each commandment, I am confident that the Sabbath commandment would rank the lowest.

All of the other commandments still garner some measure of respect among most church folks. Few Christians would dismiss the commandment about killing as a vestige of the old covenant or discount as outdated the commandment about bearing false witness. Yet the Sabbath commandment is treated differently. We commonly excerpt it from the rest of the Ten, and put it in the attic with other things we've outgrown. We know we still should not worship other gods, misuse the Lord's name, or commit adultery, but the Sabbath has been put away with the mothballs.

There's a saying that people vote with either their feet or their pocketbooks. And that may be the best measure of our imaginary poll. Rather than guessing what people would say about the continuing relevance of each of the Ten Commandments, we might simply observe what they do. I expect that, by that measure, the Sabbath commandment ranks very low in most American churches and homes.

Beyond the Commandment

We've been thinking about the Sabbath commandment within the immediate context of the Ten Commandments, but let us zoom back the lens and see the Sabbath within a larger framework.

In my experience, the Sabbath commandment is often lumped together with the dietary code of the Old Testament. It is commonly dismissed by Christians as a peculiarly Jewish relic, like the kosher laws, that has no relevance to Christian living. Such a conclusion, however, seems to me to be unjustified by Scripture.

Notice that we are not first introduced to the Sabbath at Mount Sinai along with the rest of the material we are calling "the Law." No, long before Moses, the Tabernacle, or the regulations about clean and unclean foods, we are introduced to the Sabbath in the Creation story. "And by the seventh day God completed His work which He had done; and He rested on the seventh day from all His work which He had done. Then God blessed the seventh day and sanctified it, because in it He rested from all His work which God had created and made" (Genesis 2:2-3).

It is ironic that we so commonly dismiss the Sabbath as an outdated part of the Law since the Sabbath actually predates the Law. Indeed, before there was even sin in the world, God had hallowed the seventh day. The Sabbath is introduced to us, therefore, as part of the original equipment of the universe. And the commandment is merely that we should keep holy what the Lord has made holy.

Jewish philosopher and theologian Abraham Joshua Heschel, in his insightful little volume on the Sabbath, observes that the Creation story does not attribute holiness to any space or place. There is no holy mountain and no altar. The heavens are not called holy, and neither are the human beings freshly made in God's image. "One of the most distinguished words in the Bible," Heschel writes, "is the word qadosh, holy; a word which more than any other is representative of the mystery and majesty of the divine."[1] And that is the uniquely important and meaningful word that is applied to the seventh day.

Later in the Law, of course, a number of days are identified as holy days. We explored one of them together in the previous chapter.

---

1   Abraham Joshua Heschel, *The Sabbath* (New York: Farrar, Straus and Giroux, 1951, 2005), 9.

Yet Heschel notes that the Sabbath is still qualitatively different from the others. Unlike the other holy days, "the Sabbath is entirely independent of the month and unrelated to the moon. Its date is not determined by any event in nature, such as the new moon, but by the act of creation. Thus the essence of the Sabbath is completely detached from the world of space."[2]

While it stands distinct in that way from the other holy days, the Sabbath also percolates through those other days. For the Sabbath is the starting place for Israel's holy days, the baseline for how they celebrated sacred occasions. The first and last days of the Festival of Booths, for example, were to be set aside as "a holy convocation," and on those days the people were to "do no laborious work of any kind" (Leviticus 23:35-36). Likewise at the beginning and the end of the festival surrounding Passover (Numbers 28:18, 25). So, too, on the first day of the Festival of Weeks (Number 28:26) and on the day of the Festival of Trumpets (Numbers 29:1). And, finally, the Lord taught the people that the Day of Atonement "is to be a sabbath of complete rest to you" (Leviticus 23:32).

We widen the lens a bit more, and we see that the ripples of the Sabbath extend beyond just a given week or just a given year. Indeed, the Sabbath extends beyond just God's people. It applies also to God's land.

"When you come into the land which I shall give you," the Lord told children of Israel, "then the land shall have a sabbath to the LORD." And the law for the land reads very much like the law for the people. "Six years you shall sow your field, and six years you shall prune your vineyard and gather in its crop, but during the seventh year the land shall have a sabbath rest, a sabbath to the LORD; you shall not sow your field nor prune your vineyard" (Leviticus 25:2-4).

Near the other end of Old Testament history, we learn that the Israelites failed to keep this commandment from God. We can

---

2   Heschel, *The Sabbath*, 10.

easily imagine how, one farmer at a time, one year at a time, this decision would be made. "Why should I let my land sit idle for an entire year?" they must have reasoned. "Who can afford to do that?" And so the people neglected the law of the land. But the prophet Jeremiah warned them that defeat, destruction, and exile would come their way "until the land had enjoyed its sabbaths. All the days of its desolation it kept sabbath until seventy years were complete" (2 Chronicles 36:21).

We see, then, that the Sabbath command is not a small, obscure detail in the Law. Rather, it is woven all through the Law. And, from the beginning, God weaves a Sabbath rest into creation itself.

The Day Before

Holidays have their own names, and each is associated with an identifiable date. Independence Day, Valentine's Day, Christmas Day, your birthday, your anniversary—these are all dates that can be circled on your calendar. The telling dynamic of holidays, though, is that while they are identified with specific dates, often they cannot be confined to one day. Christmas, after all, commands an entire season. And we are well-acquainted with the anticipation and preparation that precede Thanksgiving, a child's birthday, or a major anniversary.

And then there is this fascinating phenomenon: some holidays are so potent that they turn the day before into a holiday as well. Technically, December 25th is the holiday, but see how many cherished traditions, experiences, and memories surround December 24th, Christmas Eve. Likewise, New Year's Day is the legal holiday on the calendar, but so much of the festivity is tied to New Year's Eve. And the days right before both Ash Wednesday and All Saints' Day have, for better or worse, evolved into their own holidays altogether— Mardi Gras and Halloween.

A holiday, we discover, is such a potent thing that it impacts the days around it. It shouldn't surprise us, therefore, that something as profound as the Sabbath would also have an influence beyond its own twenty-four hours. And that influence is reflected both in the commandment and in the tradition.

The commandment, you recall, is not limited to the Sabbath day. That's where it begins—"Remember the sabbath day, to keep it holy" (Exodus 20:8)—but that is not where it remains. "Six days you shall labor and do all your work, but the seventh day is a sabbath of the LORD your God; *in it* you shall not do any work" (Exodus 20:9-10).

The Sabbath rules the entire week, you see. The influence of the seventh day dictates to the preceding six days. The Sabbath rest requires six days of work.

Many a busy person—or busy temperament—finds it inconceivable to take an entire day for rest. Indeed, so many souls in our present culture find it impossible even to take an entire night's sleep for rest. They are always on the go—always doing, and restlessly thinking when they are not doing.

The Bible is clear-eyed on this matter. The Scriptures do not pretend that we have nothing to do or that unplugging for a day is easy for us to do. And so the proper sense of preparation is built into the very commandment: "Six days you shall labor and do all your work." Heschel notes: "The duty to work for six days is just as much a part of God's covenant with man as the duty to abstain from work on the seventh day."[3]

This brings us to the tradition. While the commandment explicitly stipulates the impact of the Sabbath on the other six days of the week, a later tradition implies the impact of the Sabbath on the day before. "Sabbath Eve," if you will, had become its own sort of holiday with its own name.

---

3   Heschel, *Sabbath*, 28.

The detail may slip by us, for when we read it we are busy thinking about other things. The Gospel writer Mark is the one who offers us the insight. But since it comes in the midst of the story of Good Friday and Easter, we are likely to miss what is revealed about the Sabbath.

We understand that Jesus was crucified on a Friday afternoon. Saturday would have been the Jewish Sabbath. And then he was raised "very early on the first day of the week" (Mark 16:2). Mark reports that, after Jesus had died on that Friday afternoon, "because it was the Preparation Day, that is, the day before the Sabbath, Joseph of Arimathea, a prominent council member, who was himself waiting for the kingdom of God, coming and taking courage, went in to Pilate and asked for the body of Jesus" (Mark 15:42-43 NKJV).

"Preparation Day"—or, as some translations render it, the Day of Preparation—was the name for the day before the Sabbath. This was the dramatic impact of the Sabbath: that it required a day of preparation. And that fact may provide a clue as to why we don't properly honor the Sabbath: we don't prepare for it.

We know all about preparations. Think of how much preparing you do, for example, prior to taking a week of vacation. So much planning, arranging, and packing. And most of us have discovered that we are superheroes of productivity on the days just prior to leaving town.

We also know about preparing for holidays. Think of the shopping and decorating that we do before Christmas. Or the hours—perhaps days—of house cleaning and meal prep that precede Thanksgiving Day.

It should not surprise us, then, that something as significant as a holy day requires some preparation on our part. Preparation comes with the territory of that which is special, that which is important, and that which we take seriously. And so the original commandment included the matter-of-fact preparation of "six days you shall labor and do all your work." And the later tradition recognized that the day before the Sabbath was, necessarily, a day of preparation.

You and I would do well to consider what it means for a day to be made holy by God. Then, what it means for us to remember that it is holy and treat it that way. And, finally, what preparations will be required of us in order to do right by God's holy day.

"Because God Said So"

I have five children, and each of them has asked the question *why* somewhere along the way. It has not come at the same time for all of them, or about the same thing, or asked with the same tone of voice. But they have all asked *why* about some rule of mine. Why do I have to put on this uncomfortable seat belt? Why can't I wear that outfit? Why do I have to be home so early when others can stay out later? And so on.

Sometimes the *why* is asked out of curiosity with an eagerness to learn and to know. Other times it is asked with resistance and a readiness to argue. One way or the other, though, I suspect it is a universal experience for parents that their children ask the *why* question about their rules.

For generations, the parental response has often been, "Because I said so." To the average adolescent, that sounds more like a cop-out than a reason. In truth, however, it is a profoundly correct reason. The reason I make a rule and the reason my child obeys that rule, after all, do not need to be identical. She may not be capable of understanding the former, and so that cannot be the basis for the latter.

One time, years ago, when one of my children was debating some rule of the house with me, I sat down with her in her room, holding a handful of pennies. I put one penny on her toy bench, and next to that one penny I spread out a row of seven pennies. "Your little sister is just one year old," I told her, pointing to the one penny. "But you are seven years old," pointing to the longer line of coins. "How much more do you know than she does? How many things do you understand that she doesn't understand?"

She was not an enthusiastic participant in the exercise, for she sensed that it was going to work against her. Nevertheless, we identified quite a list of things that a seven-year-old knows and understands that a one-year-old does not. And then I began to spread out next to her seven pennies a long line of thirty-nine pennies. Of course it dwarfed the row of seven. "This is how old I am," I explained. "Do you see that there may be some things your daddy knows and understands that perhaps you do not?"

So it is with us and God. "Because God said so" is precisely the right reason that we should obey. This is not a heavy-handed stifling of the human creature. It is, rather, a proper recognition of God's wisdom and a magnificent opportunity for us to benefit from it.

"No amount of human knowledge, even when it approximates full capacity, is complete," write Wayne Martindale, Jerry Root, and Linda Washington in their book on C. S. Lewis. "Nevertheless, if the commands of God are given by virtue of his infinite knowledge, then every act of obedience accesses for the faithful the benefits of God's omniscience. Obedience makes it possible to live life better than we could live it on our own."[4]

So it is that I have explained to my children that the reason they obey a rule and the reason I make a rule may not be the same. "Because I said so" is a perfectly good and right reason for them to obey. Nevertheless, when it is appropriate, I also teach them along the way the reasoning at my end—why I make the rules that I do. And God has given us this gift with respect to the Sabbath command.

---

4   Wayne Martindale, Jerry Root, and Linda Washington, *The Soul of C. S. Lewis* (Carol Stream, IL: Tyndale House Publishers, 2010), 32.

At some level, of course, our generation should require less explanation of the Sabbath than any previous generation in human history. Our scientific knowledge is so much greater and our understanding of the human creature so much deeper. Do we really need to be convinced, therefore, about the rationale for rest? Experts from all sorts of fields would give us a list of chemical, nutritional, psychological, mental, and relational reasons why rest is important.

Beyond all of those, though, the Lord God offers two theological reasons for the Sabbath command.

In the Exodus account of the Ten Commandments, the Sabbath command includes this rationale: "For in six days the LORD made the heavens and the earth, the sea and all that is in them, and rested on the seventh day; therefore the LORD blessed the sabbath day and made it holy" (Exodus 20:11).

The Sabbath, then, resonates with a principle we have seen before. The Sabbath is yet one more contribution to a recurring theme. God intends for us to be like him. We see it at Creation. We see it in the command to holiness. We see it as the underlying rationale for so much of the Law. And we see it in the teachings of Jesus and the writings of the apostles. To work six days and to rest on the Sabbath, then, is to imitate God, to follow the example and the pace set by our Maker.

But there is still more. While in Exodus we read the account of God giving the Ten Commandments to Moses, in Deuteronomy we read the account of Moses recalling those commandments for the people. And in that retelling, we discover a second theological reason for the rule. "And you shall remember that you were a slave in the land of Egypt, and the LORD your God brought you out of there by a mighty hand and by an outstretched arm; therefore the LORD your God commanded you to observe the sabbath day" (Deuteronomy 5:15).

See how the Sabbath is a benefit *and* a reminder of their liberation? There had been a time for the children of Israel when their labor was forced. They belonged to others, and so they worked when they were commanded by their taskmasters to work, perhaps without any days of rest. But now, the Lord has set them free from their bondage. Now they no longer belong to their labor. Now they belong to God. And their new Master commands them to rest.

One further word deserves to be said on this point—an etymological consideration.

Ancient Hebrew was the original language of most of the Old Testament. And in ancient Hebrew, most words are built upon three-letter roots. Slight changes in vowels, in prefixes, and in suffixes, then, give nuance and precision to the meaning of the words, but the original three-letter root remains the starting place for many derivatives.

We might illustrate the principle with our English word *just*. See how we build on that basic root to create other, related words. Justice. Unjust. Justify. Injustice. Justiciable. The single root word gives rise to many derivatives.

In biblical Hebrew, there is a root word that we might transliterate in English as *abd*. The derivatives of that root include the Hebrew words for work, servant, slave, bondage, serve, and worship. See, then, the larger theme involved in Israel's story and their relationship with God. They were once *abd* in Egypt (Deuteronomy 6:21), but the Lord set them free. Now, they belong to God, and central to their covenant with him is their observance of a holy day when they will stop their *abd* in order to rest (Deuteronomy 5:13). And in this new covenant freedom, they are to *abd* the Lord with gladness (Psalm 100:2) and to *abd* him only (Deuteronomy 6:13).

During a Sunday school class in a church I served years ago, a couple of the men were discussing their work lives. They were both executives with big companies in town. They dressed well, they traveled a great deal, they had impressive offices, and they lived in very nice homes. But as they talked about their work, one smiled and said, "We're really just well-paid slaves, you know. We belong to the company. What we do, where we go, where our family lives—it's all up to the company."

In various ways, we continue to run the risk of belonging to our work. But the Lord our God does not intend for us to belong to anyone or anything else. And the Sabbath becomes a living symbol of the truth that we do not belong to any other master, including our work. We belong to the God who sets us free.

T.G.I.S.

We have four children still at home. Two are teenagers, and the other two are preschoolers. And I observe in these very different stages somewhat different attitudes toward the idea of bedtime.

The younger children, as you might expect, sometimes resist going to bed. They want to stay up and keep playing. Yet in parenting them we tend to insist on bedtime in its literal sense; that is, there is a time at which they need to go to bed.

With our teenagers, we allow more latitude and self-determination. And because they have more responsibilities and schoolwork, I observe in them an attitude toward bedtime that is often more typical of adults. Bedtime is not so much a fixed time as it is the thing that happens when the work is done.

I lived that way for a lot of years. Sleep was routinely postponed until the work was done. But I found that this was a miserable system, for there was always more work to do. And so I went to bed late, exhausted, and with reluctance. In more recent years, however, I have rediscovered the wisdom that we insist on with young children. There is a time at which I ought to go to bed, and I endeavor to keep it as I would any other appointment. This is, I find, a much more restful and healthy way to live.

And this is, of course, what is built into nature. The sun goes down. The lights in our room, as it were, are turned off. And so we know it is time for sleep. Except that in our modern age electricity has allowed and encouraged us to circumvent nature and keep our lights on well into the night.

What is true in the relation between work and rest at the end of every day is also true at the end of every week. Will we rest on the Sabbath because the time for rest has come? Or will we postpone our rest indefinitely until our work is done? The latter will not prove to be a recipe for rest. And it betrays the system that God has put in place.

In Jewish tradition, based on Scripture, a day begins at sundown. So, for our purposes, Tuesday does not begin whenever we awaken on Tuesday morning. And it does not begin at the stroke of midnight between Monday and Tuesday. Rather, Tuesday begins at sundown on what we think of as Monday evening. Consequently, the Sabbath began at sundown on Friday night.

To return to a discussion of *Fiddler on the Roof*, we observe the life of a Jewish family in early twentieth-century Russia. And early in the film, we see that family preparing for the Sabbath. It is Friday afternoon, and everyone is scurrying around, completing their chores, and keeping an eye on the setting sun, which will determine their time to begin their rest. The Sabbath is like a wise bedtime—an appointment to be kept.

When I was a kid living at home, a customary part of our Sundays at home was that my dad would lie down on the living room sofa and take a Sunday afternoon nap. It was not a long nap, but it was clearly refreshing to him. He enjoyed it, and he looked forward to it. And I remember one day, as he settled himself down on the sofa, hearing him say, "It is time for my scheduled luxury!"

The phrase was just right, for both words were true. His Sunday afternoon nap was, indeed, scheduled. It was a fixed part of his pattern. And it was also a luxury—a small indulgence that he greatly enjoyed.

And so it should be with us and the Sabbath. It is a scheduled luxury. It is a good gift from God that is built into the pattern of each week.

Like the bell that rings at the end of the school day or the whistle that blows to signal the end of work at the plant, let the start of the Sabbath thrill our hearts. Let us call the Sabbath a delight (Isaiah 58:13), and enjoy it as such. Let us faithfully treat as holy what God has made holy. Let us follow the pace that our Maker has set. And let us live as people that the Lord has set free to worship him.

11

Cleanliness Is Next to Godliness

You are to distinguish between the holy and the common,
between the unclean and the clean.
Leviticus 10:10 NRSV

The chapter's title is not actually found in the Bible, but it could be. And if it were, it would be in the Old Testament Law. For in the Law, the principle is spelled out in multiple ways that cleanliness is, indeed, next to godliness.

That was a favorite expression of earlier generations. I don't think it is said as commonly anymore, though not because we are less concerned with cleanliness. Indeed, our generation is in a better position than perhaps any before to appreciate the Law's insistence on cleanliness. While we are better acquainted with being sanitary, I wonder if we have lost some sense for being godly. If so, then we will not naturally see the important connection between the two.

In this chapter, we will endeavor to reestablish that connection. Let us build on what we already have: a strong sense for the importance of cleanliness. And then let us rediscover the beauty and importance of godliness, and how cleanliness is a step in that direction.

Ahead of Their Time

Perhaps more than any generation before, twenty-first-century Americans should sympathize with the Levitical cleanliness code. We have in our day such a host of policies, regulations, and best practices in place for our restaurants, our hospitals, and our manufacturing. The grocery store where I shop even offers wipes that a person might use to clean the handle of the shopping cart before we use it.

Have we just become persnickety? Are we all germophobes? In some individual cases, perhaps. But there is much more involved than just idiosyncratic habits.

As a pastor, I am regularly visiting in hospitals, and you can hardly visit a modern American hospital without being impressed by the importance of cleanliness. The masks, gloves, and gowns; the hairnets and ubiquitous hand sanitizers—these are the tacit reminders of the relationship between cleanliness and health. And, on the larger stage of society, our various environmental protection efforts also bear witness to our contemporary understanding of that relationship.

But that understanding was slow to come, and a great price was paid along the way. Ignaz Semmelweis, a Hungarian doctor, is sometimes referred to as the father of hand washing. Semmelweis observed a much higher survival rate of mothers and their newborns in one particular maternity ward than in another one in the very same hospital. He conducted experiments to try to discern the critical difference between the two, and after much trial and error, discovered that the patients falling ill had been treated by doctors who also had performed autopsies. He recommended that the doctors in the one ward be careful to wash their hands and instruments in a chlorine solution before dealing with their patients, and the death rate on that ward fell dramatically. It seems like a stunningly obvious solution to us, yet those unnecessary deaths were not happening in some backward hospital in an underdeveloped country marked more by superstition than science. No, Semmelweis's story comes from mid-nineteenth-century Europe.[1]

With divine guidance, ancient Israel had a sense for the importance of cleanliness three thousand years earlier. The Law did not call for bleeding out evil humours, waving magic wands, or wearing charms to ward off malevolent spirits. Rather, even in that ancient context, we observe an insistence on washing, an awareness of contagion, a concern for public health, a practice of quarantining, a sensitivity to bodily fluids, and a conspicuous emphasis on cleanliness.

I recognize that the Israelites of Moses' generation did not have a fraction of the scientific knowledge that we enjoy. But that is what makes the Law all the more remarkable to me. Even in an age that so predated our modern understanding of how the world works, still they were instructed in practices that helped to keep them healthy.

In the twenty-first century, our doctors and nurses, dental hygienists, and even trainers on the sidelines of a football field are equipped with gloves and masks, and we might assume this is a trend of the twenty-first century. Yet three millennia ago, Israel was already being careful about blood and semen and spit. Similarly, today we have abundant scientific data about the negative impact of mold and mildew in one's living space, something we might attribute

---

1   Rebecca Davis, "The Doctor Who Championed Hand-Washing and Briefly Saved Lives," National Public Radio, January 12, 2015, https://www.npr.org/sections/health -shots/2015/01/12/375663920/the-doctor-who-championed-hand-washing-and-saved -women-s-lives.

to modern-day scientific tools and knowledge. Yet long ago, the priests of Israel were helping homeowners to identify and clean up unwholesome spots on their walls.

Ancient Israel was ahead of its time, and that is due to the Law of God. In every respect, the Law that God gave his people was for their good. It kept them clean. It kept them healthy. And it steered them toward godliness.

Care Instructions

They come with every purchase. Whether it is the tag inside a new article of clothing or a page in the manual that comes with a new appliance, they are there. The "care instructions" accompany your new furniture, your new phone, your new car, and your new television. The question is how best to take care of this good new thing, and a part of the answer is always how to clean it.

I confess that I don't pay much attention to the care instructions at first. In my excitement about the new thing, I want to get on with using it, and cleaning it seems a very remote concern. When the thing is brand-new, it is unblemished and perfect. Why bother with reading about how to clean it?

But the manufacturer knows that it won't stay clean. The clothes will get dirty, the screen will get dusty, and so you and I need to know how best to clean the thing. I shouldn't clean my suit the same way I clean my car, which is also different from how I clean my laptop, which is also different from how I clean my teeth.

Interestingly, the instructions about cleaning are not called "cosmetic instructions" but "care instructions." Keeping the thing clean is not just a superficial enterprise. It's not just about keeping the thing looking as pretty as possible, though that is often our motivation. In reality, though, to keep a thing clean is to care for it—to make sure that it stays in good working order.

The cleanliness code in the Book of Leviticus, therefore, should not be seen as an onerous thing, but as helpful, even essential. They have been favored by God with care instructions for things that matter—their bodies, their homes, and God's dwelling in their midst. And central to caring for those things was to keep them clean.

Of course, cleaning is not a once-and-for-all achievement. This is a realization that every child tasked with making his or her bed quickly discovers and enunciates. "Why should I bother making it when I'm just going to mess it up again?" So it goes. To clean a thing is not a one-time task. It is a recurring obligation. It is a function of care and maintenance.

Accordingly, the care instructions reflect a matter-of-fact realism about life in this world. The dentist does not send you out the door after a teeth cleaning with some Pollyannaish expectation that you'll never need to come back again. Quite the contrary. He or she will assume that you will need to be back again for another cleaning six months later.

The Law, likewise, does not cross its fingers and hope you and I will never get soiled. Leviticus isn't shocked by uncleanness, but, rather, prescribes the steps to restore cleanness, knowing full well that we need to be cleaned again and again.

Notably, the holiest day on the Hebrew calendar—Yom Kippur, or the Day of Atonement—was a sort of annual cleaning day. We think of it as a highly spiritual day, and rightly so. Yet Hebrew scholar Jacob Milgrom notes that the underlying Hebrew word, *kaphar* (from which comes our Kippur), "seems to derive from a concrete notion of rubbing clean."[2]

The physical imagery employed for spiritual reality is not confined to the Old Testament Law. The physical is a helpful visual to

---

2   Robert Alter, *The Five Books of Moses: A Translation with Commentary* (New York: W.W. Norton, 2004), 612.

give us understanding of the spiritual. And so we recall Jesus bending down to wash his disciples' feet. Peter's first objection was to the Master's doing servant's work at all. But then, in characteristic fashion, Peter swings wildly to the other extreme, saying, "Lord, then wash not only my feet, but also my hands and my head" (John 13:9). But Jesus replies, "He who has bathed needs only to wash his feet" (v. 10). It is, for the moment, an entirely pragmatic statement and is limited to the physical realm. But then Jesus extends the meaning to the rest of the disciples, saying, "You are clean, but not all of you." And then the narrator connects the dots for us: "For He knew the one who was betraying him; for this reason he said, 'Not all of you are clean'" (v. 11).

Peter, you see, is clean, but Judas is not. Has Peter bathed more recently? No, the image of cleanliness has been turned inside out. Peter is clean on the inside, while Judas is not. And it is that sober reality that makes the hymn writer earnestly cry out to God, "Make and keep me pure within."[3]

If I am going to care well for the things that belong to me—my clothes, my computer, my car, or my soul—then I must understand the care instructions for each. And those will include knowing how to make and keep the thing clean. God wanted the ancient people of Israel to have a passion for cleanliness. And God's Law continues to be a tutor for us in this as well.

Is "Unclean" Unfair?

We have this picture in our minds of the leper having to self-identify by calling out, "Unclean!" Perhaps we have an impression that the Law fomented an unhelpful attitude toward women and their menstrual cycles. And we wonder if the Law's prescribed distinction between "clean" and "unclean" was a negative thing.

---

3   Charles Wesley, "Jesus, Lover of My Soul," *The United Methodist Hymnal*, 479.

I believe that Jesus' words to Peter in that New Testament story can help us to understand the cleanliness code of the Old Testament Law: "He who has bathed needs only to wash his feet."

It is a practical recognition of how life in this world works: even a clean person is likely to get dirty feet.

That was a day of dirt roads and sandals, of course, and for most folks it was also a day of walking wherever you went. It was almost impossible, therefore, to come to the end of a day without needing to wash your feet. They would have been thick with the dust and dirt of the day's work and walking. And so Jesus was conceding that, even if Peter's body has been recently bathed, he still needed his feet to be washed.

See that there is no condemnation in that. Dirty feet come with the territory. The dirty-footed disciple is not to be scolded, therefore, just washed. And that is the attitude we should recognize in the Old Testament Law. To call something unclean was not necessarily a condemnation or a value judgment. It was simply a recognition of the facts, and the goal was to get the unclean thing cleaned up again.

A great variety of things were identified as "unclean" in the Old Testament Law. A skin disease might label a person as unclean, yet that was not a moral failure. Leprosy does not equal sin. But the Law recognized that, for the sake of the larger community, the uncleanness needed to be monitored and quarantined.

Certain foods were also identified as "unclean" for the ancient people of Israel, and many of those standards remain in force for observant Jews today who are careful about a kosher diet. Various traditions and interpretations have been offered through the years about the rationale behind some of these restrictions. Were they motivated by health concerns? Was the goal for the Israelites to distinguish themselves from the practices of the peoples around them? Were there taboos associated with certain creatures—

carnivores and scavengers, for example—or animals that seemed to be "a violation of appropriate categories"?[4] The reasons are unclear, and Christians understand that these restrictions have been removed by Christ (Mark 7:19). Nevertheless, the regulations serve to remind us that all of life, right down to our eating and drinking, may be done to the glory of God (1 Corinthians 10:31).

Perhaps most telling of all, though, is the fact that some natural bodily functions also made a person "unclean." A woman's menstruation, for example, or a man's emission of semen. Inasmuch as these are part of God's design, we are guaranteed that "unclean" is not a moral judgment in the Law. Rather, like the disciples' dirty feet, it is a fact of life. It comes with the territory of life in this world. And so the Law is not condemning—just diagnosing and prescribing.

The cleanliness code in the Law may bring to mind the doctrine of original sin. Unlike the actual bad choices that I have made and my own personal failures, original sin does not have my fingerprints on it. On the contrary, it has its fingerprints on me. It is a fact of life in this fallen world. And the cleanliness code reminds me that the Lord wants me to be clean and provides the means for that to happen.

I am reminded of occasions when, as a young boy, I would come into the house filthy from a long summer day of playing outside. My mom would typically stop me at the door, saying, "Don't bring that mess into my house!" But that didn't mean that she sent me back out of the house, forever to wallow in my dirt. No, she lovingly and thoroughly cleaned me up!

The Law, likewise, impressed upon the people of Israel that they were not to bring uncleanness into God's house. But the Lord did not just leave them in their uncleanness. Cleanliness is next to godliness, and so the Lord provided for their cleansing so that they could come near to him.

---

4   Alter, *The Five Books of Moses*, 951

A Suitable Place to Live and Work

I have spent my life living with two women—my mother and then my wife—who are definitely cut from the same cloth. They both like to have things "just so": clean and orderly, a place for everything, and everything in its place. And I have discovered, from living with each of them, that cleaning comes first. Cleaning comes before living, and cleaning comes before working.

When I was a boy, my parents owned a summer cottage near a lake in western New York State, and our family would spend the month of July there together each summer. Now, driving all the way from Wisconsin to New York with two kids, in July, and with no air conditioning in the car, can make for a long trip. But each year we would do it. And each year, we would finally pull up in front of our cottage hot, tired, and really ready to get out of the car.

I remember well what my sister and I wanted to do as soon as we arrived: to get out and go! We were so excited about being back in that favorite spot that we wanted, right away, to get out of the car and reacquaint ourselves with a place that we loved. And in retrospect, I can guess that my parents longed for the opposite upon arrival: to sit down and put up their feet, perhaps have a bite to eat, and maybe take a shower or a nap.

But my mom had a different agenda. Before anyone could do anything else, the first thing we all had to do was clean.

The house had been closed up all fall, winter, and spring, you see. All sorts of cobwebs had accumulated on the porch, on the windows, and in the corners. All the dishes and utensils needed to be washed after sitting in drawers and cupboards all winter. The floors needed to be swept, the rugs vacuumed, the bathrooms scrubbed, and the beds made. Then we could live there. Then we could go and play and explore and enjoy. But the cleaning came first. My mom just couldn't live in a place until it was clean.

My wife, Karen, meanwhile, can't concentrate in a place until it's clean. Now, this is a great inconvenience, and she would admit that it is, but it's just how she is. So, for example, if Karen has a letter to write, she cannot easily take pen in hand if there are dishes waiting in the sink or dirty laundry in the hamper. Likewise in our early years of marriage, when we were both still finishing our schooling, the apartment had to be clean and orderly in order for Karen to be able to focus on reading or writing or studying. It's not that she is a compulsive cleaner, it's just that she requires a clean environment for her to do her work.

We all need a suitable place to live and work. For different people that means different things, of course, but we all have some kind of preferred environment. We all have our sense for what makes a place "just so," and so does God. Indeed, that trait within us may be one of the ways that we are made in God's image.

More than anyone, the Lord demonstrates and articulates a desire for everything to be "just so." From Eden to the Tabernacle to heaven, we see evidence of that desire. Just as surely as you or I require a suitable place to live and work, I believe that God does too!

We read a rather graphic illustration of that fact in Deuteronomy 23, where the Lord actually instructs the people on their bathroom habits. In simple summary, the instruction for Israel's army was to designate a place outside the camp where they would relieve themselves. And, specifically, they were to take with them a tool so that they could dig a hole, and then cover the waste with dirt when they were done.

Years ago, when I was leading a group of folks in a study of the Old Testament, we came across this passage. The next week, a man from the class handed me a playful note, which asked: "Do we really suppose that this commandment was given by God, who moved about the Israelite camp in a pillar of cloud and fire, or by Moses, who had to walk around the camp in open-toed sandals?"

Well, the fact is that God gave the people the rationale for this commode commandment. "Keep your camp ritually clean, because the LORD your God is with you in your camp to protect you and to give you victory over your enemies. Do not do anything indecent that would cause the LORD to turn his back on you" (Deuteronomy 23:14 GNT).

That's the reason. The reason why the people of Israel were instructed to be particular about their bathroom habits was that the Lord was in their camp with them. The rationale was not to make the Israelite camp more civil, more sanitary, or more pleasant for the other people. Those were happy byproducts, but the expressed purpose was to keep the camp clean because God was there. In short, the purpose of the command was to make the Israelite camp a suitable place for God to live and work.

I'm afraid our contemporary theology may be deficient on this point. We dismiss as primitive any suggestion of a localized god. We affirm the omnipresence of God, and so we reject any suggestion that the Lord is somehow confined to a particular, physical location— whether that is Sinai, the Holy of Holies, or Zion. But in our denial of God being exclusively present in certain places, we may lose sight of the biblical testimony that God is especially present in certain places.

What places? Suitable places!

One day, the Lord showed the prophet Ezekiel some of the idolatrous practices that were taking place within the temple precincts in Jerusalem. "Do you see what is happening?" the Lord asked the prophet. "Look at the disgusting things the people of Israel are doing here, driving me farther and farther away from my holy place" (Ezekiel 8:6 GNT). The behavior of the people, you see, disgusted God. And that behavior provoked the Lord to remove his presence from that place. The very house of God itself was no longer a suitable place for God to live and work.

And so the Law tutored the people to think in terms of purity. Make the dwelling place of God a suitable place for God. For them, that had implications for their campsite. For you and me, it has implications for our hearts.

Mildew and Salvation

Among the least appealing sections in the Old Testament Law for me are Leviticus chapters 12 through 15. There we read detailed instructions concerning diseased flesh, mildew, and bodily discharges. We read of yellowish hairs, red spots, and spreading decay. It is not mealtime reading for me. And yet, I embrace and celebrate the wisdom that I find in those chapters. For their message to me is not ultimately medical, but theological. The issue is not merely unclean and clean, but sin and salvation.

Take, for example, the instructions given to an Israelite who finds a spot of something on the wall of their house (Leviticus 14:33-57). The exact nature of the spot is uncertain. The King James Version and New American Standard Bible, for example, translate it as "leprosy." The Revised Standard Version calls it "some sort of disease." We will follow the New International Version and Good News Translation, which plausibly think of it as "mold" and "mildew" respectively.

In my experience, the common human reflex is to try to hide or cover spots. Whether a blemish on one's skin, a stain on one's clothing, or a mess in one's house, we do our best to keep other people from seeing it. Yet the Law required the Israelites to do precisely the opposite. Rather than pushing a piece of furniture in front of the unsightly and embarrassing spot, they were to call in the priest to examine it.

What follows, then, is a careful process of monitoring and cleaning. Together, the priest and the homeowner walk through a series of steps to try to guarantee the cleanliness of the house. The perfect picture is for the uncleanness to be successfully removed from the house. Yet the procedures are no-nonsense in doing whatever is necessary to remove the uncleanness.

As unappetizing or even pedantic as this material may be to read, I recognize the truth in it.

I recognize the truth that a little impurity does not stay a little impurity. Our instinct for avoidance tempts us to overlook a small problem or concern. And so if I find a small spot on my wall, I might reason that I don't need to bother about it, for it's not that big a deal. But a little mildew doesn't stay a little mildew. A little tooth decay doesn't stay a little tooth decay. A little rust doesn't stay a little rust. A little cancer doesn't stay a little cancer. And a little sin doesn't stay a little sin. The Law challenges me to deal with the spot.

I also recognize the truth of accountability. I don't really want anyone else to see my spots. I'd rather take care of it myself. But the Law tells me that I need to bring someone else in to monitor and to help me get it cleaned. James says, "Confess your sins to one another" (5:16), contrary to all of our preferences to hide what is unsightly and embarrassing. Yet the apostle's purpose is not embarrassment but healing. "Confess your sins to one another, and pray for one another, so that you may be healed," he writes. The rationale of the Old Testament Law and the New Testament instruction are the same: bring in someone else to help get rid of the uncleanness.

And I recognize, too, the no-nonsense response to uncleanness. The priest would require me to scrape, to dig out, to re-plaster, or perhaps even to tear down. It all seems rather drastic. But the dentist and the oncologist will also, in their arenas, recommend drastic action to stem the spread. And Jesus teaches me to be just as intolerant in response to sin. "If your right eye makes you stumble, tear it out and throw it from you; for it is better for you to lose one of the parts of your body, than for your whole body to be thrown into hell. If your right hand makes you stumble, cut it off and throw it from you;

for it is better for you to lose one of the parts of your body, than for your whole body to go into hell" (Matthew 5:29-30).

Saturday Cleanup

For all of my growing up years, my dad served as a pastor and preacher in local churches—first in Madison, Wisconsin, and then in Cleveland, Ohio. He worked hard all week, but Sundays were especially important and particularly demanding. And so Saturday nights in our home had a distinctive feel.

Saturday nights were stay-at-home nights. Other evenings there may have been meetings, appointments, or occasions to attend. But Saturday nights were protected. We stayed home, and we went to bed early.

There was a pervading sense in our home that the next day was Sunday, and Sunday deserved our best. Granted, it was a uniquely demanding day for the preacher in the family, but the prospect of Sunday impacted the whole family, not just him. We were all getting ready for Sunday.

And it was more than just going to bed early. I remember that Saturday was the day my dad would shine his shoes (or pay me to do it). He would often get his car washed that day as well. And back home, Saturday night was always bath night for me, whether I needed it or not. As a young boy, I disliked taking baths, and it was a point of contention on other days or nights. But on Saturday night, it was nonnegotiable. And, as I recall, Saturday night was also when my mom would clip my nails.

I don't remember any single occasion when my father or my mother fully explained our Saturday night patterns. Perhaps they did. I do remember, though, that my mom would respond to any *why* with the simple reminder that "Tomorrow is Sunday" or "We've got church tomorrow."

That little bit of perspective combined with the family practices to make an impression on me. Something about Sundays and church deserved our best. More to the point, God deserved our best. And part of "best" was to be clean.

We know how that looks in other areas of life. When guests are coming, a primary preparation is cleaning. And when the occasion is a special one, we make sure our clothes, our shoes, and our bodies are clean. Cleaning is part of how we prepare for many important things, and cleanliness is part of how we honor certain people and occasions. It made perfect sense, therefore, that my parents should make sure everyone and everything was clean for Sunday.

Clean and Home on a Saturday Night

It wasn't until I went off to college that I began to reflect on our Saturday practices. For as long as I was living at home, I just took it for granted and never gave it much conscious thought. Once I was away from home, however, I recognized, in retrospect, the Saturday-to-Sunday culture that my parents had created.

I remember lying in bed one Saturday evening, early in my first year at college. I felt a certain homesickness, and I couldn't put my finger on it at first. Why was it suddenly more bittersweet to be away from home and family tonight than it had been any of the other days and nights that I had been away? And then I finally recognized just how different and special Saturday nights felt—everything was clean, and everyone was home.

Over the next number of years, that experience became for me an image of a deeper longing. When I went through periods of rebellion or times when I had distanced myself from God, I experienced the longing of a prodigal. And in my prayers, I expressed it as a longing for Saturday nights. I wanted to be clean, and I wanted to be home.

As with so many elements of the Law, the physical anticipates the spiritual. As Christians, we have in our hymnody so many images of washing and cleanness to express not the needs of our bodies but the realities of our souls. We recognize the dirtiness of sin, and we long to be cleansed from it. We own the impurity of our thoughts, our actions, and our motivations, and we earnestly desire to have those impurities removed from us. And so we sense the Law pointing us toward the gospel truth: that a holy God not only deserves and requires a clean people, but also provides for our cleansing.

Interestingly, in the Old Testament Law, the chief agent of cleansing was blood. Even in that context where the emphasis appeared to be primarily physical and external, still people embraced the symbolism of sprinkled blood as the essential detergent. And on this side of the cross, we know better still how true that is. And so we sing with William Cowper:

> There is a fountain filled with blood
> drawn from Emmanuel's veins;
> and sinners plunged beneath that flood
> lose all their guilty stains.
> The dying thief rejoiced to see
> that fountain in his day;
> and there may I, though vile as he,
> wash all my sins away.[5]

---

5 William Cowper, "There Is a Fountain Filled with Blood," *The United Methodist Hymnal*, 622.

12
A Good Place to Keep It

Be very careful to keep the commandment and the law
that Moses the servant of the LORD gave you.

Joshua 22:5 NIV

The milk carton reads, "Keep refrigerated." The medicine bottle reads, "Keep out of reach of children." The care and safety instructions for the computer read, "Keep away from radiators and heat sources."

Where an item is meant to be kept reveals some things about that item. Which brings us to these significant places in Scripture: a box, a tent, a valley, a throne, and a doorway. We want to visit each of those places in this chapter. And in each place, we will find God's Law.

The Box in the Tent

Our first stop is a place we've already visited together in an earlier chapter. We remember the bird's-eye view of Israel's camp and how strikingly organized it is. It is not a hodgepodge of tents, but a community neatly arranged by tribes: three to the east, three to the west, three to the north, and three to the south. And that organization naturally draws all attention to what is in the center of the camp.

At the intersection of the twelve tribes, at the hub of Israel's spokes, stands the largest tent of all. It is a gem of color in a bland landscape. It is the Tabernacle compound: God's tent set up right in the midst of the tents of God's people.

When we zoomed in for a closer look, we saw that the Tent has two sections. The Holy Place and the Most Holy Place, with a floor-to-ceiling, wall-to-wall curtain separating the two. The Holy Place featured several different items. But the Most Holy Place—the Holy of Holies—featured only one piece of furniture. It's a box, a gilded box, with carvings of angels on its lid. It was called the ark of the covenant, and it was Israel's most sacred physical object.

While the ark eventually contained several meaningful items, it was designed to contain one thing: God's Ten Commandments. Those commandments were the centerpiece of God's Law. Those commandments expressed the essence of the covenant between God and the people. And the ark that contained them was associated with the very presence of God.

At the moment in history when God gave those commandments, Israel was a people on the move. They were traveling in phases from Egypt to Canaan, camping in one place after another. Everything about their life had to remain mobile, including their place of worship. And so the Tabernacle was designed to be dismantled, carried, and set up again. And, likewise, the ark came equipped with carrying poles so that it could be easily and continually transported.

When the Israelites set up camp, the ark was not haphazardly placed or thoughtlessly parked here or there. It was assigned a specific spot—the most central and sacred spot in Israel's campsite. Physically, the ark was at the core of the community.

Meanwhile, when the Israelites broke camp and began to march, the ark assumed a different position. The ark that camped in the midst of the people traveled in front of the people. The priests carried the ark on the shoulders, and they led the way when Israel moved from site to site.

We have an idiom in our day to describe someone or something that is prominent in a given situation. We say that they are "front and center." The Law of God—as it was kept in the ark—was literally front and center for the children of Israel.

The order of the people marching when they moved and the arrangement of their campsite when they stopped was all prescribed by God. It was by God's design that the ark was front and center. And the physical location of the ark was instructive to the people about the place of God's Law in their lives.

The Valley

At the end of Moses' tenure as Israel's leader, he spoke a grand farewell to the people, which included a great many final instructions. We have a record of Moses' parting words in the Book of Deuteronomy. And along the way, Moses taught the people about a ritual they were to conduct once they had moved into the Promised Land.

The ritual was another sort of instruction about where the Law was to be kept. Just like the milk carton or the medicine bottle, Moses was clear with the people about where they should keep God's Law. And so he told them about two mountains—Ebal and Gerizim. All the words of the Law were to be inscribed on large rocks covered with plaster and installed at Mount Ebal. Six of the twelve tribes were to stand there on Mount Ebal, while the other six tribes stood across the valley on Mount Gerizim. And then, in a grand antiphonal, with the Law written out on large stones before them, the nation was to recite the consequences of disobeying God's Law and the blessings of obeying it.

The geography of ancient Israel was asymmetrical. But if you took a map of that land and attempted to draw one line straight down the approximate middle of that land from north to south, then drew another line straight across the middle from east to west, you'd be fascinated by the intersection. For those two lines would likely meet at the valley between Mount Ebal and Mount Gerizim.

Israel's campsite in the wilderness was highly symmetrical, and the Law was positioned in the center of their tent metropolis. Once in the land of Canaan, the Israelites' dwelling place was not so symmetrical anymore. And yet still, as near as possible, a great copy of the Law was to be set up in the middle of their land.

The Throne

In his farewell instructions to the people, Moses anticipated another future facet of life in their new land. He predicted that a time would come when the people would ask to have a king, just like so many of the surrounding nations. Moses did not wholeheartedly endorse such a move, but he allowed for it. And, in the spirit of the sand wedge we discussed in an earlier chapter, he gave the people instructions for how the king should function if they do have one. A king may not be the best idea for Israel, but if Israel has one, then let's at least make the best of it.

"Now it shall come about when he sits on the throne of his kingdom," Moses said of the hypothetical king, "he shall write for himself a copy of this law on a scroll in the presence of the Levitical priests. And it shall be with him, and he shall read it all the days of his life, that he may learn to fear the LORD his God, by carefully observing all the words of this law and these statutes" (Deuteronomy 17:18-19).

I expect it's an easy thing for a king to be intoxicated by his own sovereignty. From the start of his reign, therefore, and every day of it, Israel's king would be reminded that he takes his orders from the King of kings. The man who wore Israel's crown was not to look down only from his throne, but also always to look up.

You and I are not kings, but we, too, may be intoxicated by our own sovereignty. If nothing else, it is a matter of personal sovereignty for us. For even if we are not in charge of anyone or anything else, we reckon that we are in charge of ourselves. And so it is essential for us—as it was for Israel's kings—to be reminded daily that we take our orders from the King of kings.

The first step in that education of Israel's king was that he was to write out his own copy of the Law. Nothing could impress upon an individual the words and details of the Law quite like personally having to copy it over by hand. And Moses' detail that the copying was to be done "in the presence of the Levitical priests" established an appropriate sense of oversight and accountability.

I'm reminded of the checks and controls that govern the money counters at our church. No individual handles the money by himself or herself. Rather, all the counting and accounting of the church's money is done within specific guidelines in order to protect against both carelessness and mischief.

So, too, with the king's copying of the Law. The priests were in the room, overseeing the process, in order to protect against both carelessness and mischief. God's Law must not become the victim of either neglect or editing.

Then, having made for himself a copy of the Law, Moses said "it shall be with him." The king didn't just check the box of copying the Law and then move on. The book of the Law was not to be set aside on a shelf or tucked away in a drawer. God's Law was to be the king's companion.

Finally, Moses said that the king "shall read it all the days of his life." Most things that we read are one-and-done items. A few things are so worthwhile or so personally important to us that we reread them multiple times. But only God's written word can lay claim to this unique place in our lives: read it every day for the rest of your life.

Here is a book we will never outgrow. Our endeavor, rather, is to grow into it. Here is wisdom we cannot exhaust. Here is truth that will only increase in beauty over time as we come to see it more and more clearly. Israel's king, therefore, was not simply to copy the Law and then set it aside. Nor was he to give it a read-through and then move on to the next book on his shelf. No, this was a book he was never to set aside but to keep by his side for all the days of his life.

The Walls and Doors

We see the symbolic vessel for God's Law—the ark of the covenant—front and center. We see the Law's national monument centrally located at Mount Ebal. We see the royal copy of the Law kept at the king's side. But that's all a bit removed, isn't it, from the average Israelite and his family? And so let's make it more personal.

We keep the photos that are precious to us in an album. We keep the documents that are important to us in a fireproof chest or a safe deposit box. And the memorabilia that is sentimentally significant to us we keep on display on our mantels, shelves, and dressers.

Where we choose to keep certain personal items reveals something about the value and importance of those items to us. And so Moses had one other instruction for the people about where the Law was to be kept. Make sure to give it a place of value in your home.

"Recite them to your children," Moses says of God's commands, "and talk about them when you are at home and when you are away, when you lie down and when you rise. Bind them as a sign on your hand, fix them as an emblem on your forehead, and write them on the doorposts of your house and on your gates" (Deuteronomy 6:7-9 NRSV).

Did he leave anything out?

The Law of God is meant to be part of our conversation, which means part of our relationships. And see that it is not just a subject of conversation once a week in church or a Sunday school class. No, it is morning and night. It is home and away.

Furthermore, Moses invites the people to build into their lives physical reminders of God's Law. As you or I might wear a wedding ring, the people were to wear an emblem on their own bodies to remind them of the terms of their covenant with God. Their homes, too, were to bear the marks of God's Law. Like a poster on a teenager's wall or the address on your front door, reminders of God's commands were to be posted where the people would always see them. And even beyond the individual family's home, the very entrance to the city should have a sign to trigger remembrance of the things of God. Perhaps where we might have a welcome sign with the community's population, Moses would recommend a verse about loving and fearing the Lord.

Moses paints a portrait of a life and a home saturated with the word of God. We human beings, as we have noted, are creatures of time and space. Very wisely, then, Moses encourages us to build God's Law into all our times and all our spaces. If we let it percolate through all time and space of our lives, surely then our lives will be formed and guided by it.

Dr. Seuss fans will recognize a strange little character called Sam-I-Am. He is a cheerful and persistent little guy who serves as a sort of evangelist for green eggs and ham in the life of his somewhat grouchy and obstinate friend. Sam-I-Am's approach is to propose every possible setting, hoping to find some circumstance in which his friend would be willing to try green eggs and ham, but his friend is not interested.

Finally, by the end of the story, the friend's resistance is so worn down, and he agrees to try—just to try—one bite of the much ballyhooed green eggs and ham. After a moment of suspense, we see that he likes them—likes them very much! He tells of all the places he would eat them wherever he is—in a boat, with a goat, in the rain, on a train, ending with:

> "And I will eat them here and there.
> Say! I will eat them ANYWHERE!"[1]

Long before Dr. Seuss playfully rhymed this thorough devotion to green eggs and ham, Moses, in all seriousness, called upon God's people to make God's word just so ubiquitous, so versatile, and so systematically embraced in their lives.

The instruction to "keep refrigerated" speaks of something that is perishable. The instruction to "keep out of reach of children" speaks of something that is hazardous. The instruction to "keep away from radiators and out of direct sunlight" speaks of something that is a bit fragile. And, likewise, with God's word. Where it was kept tells us much about it.

The Commandments were kept in the ark of the covenant, front and center. They were copied by the king and kept at his side. Reminders of them were placed on the body of each individual, on the door of each house, and on the gate of each town. Where the Law was kept tells us much about the Law.

And so we are invited to consider the place of God's word in our lives. Does its place in my life, home, and heart suggest that it is a trivial thing or a holy thing? Is God's word peripheral, on the outskirts of my time and space, or is it front and center, and daily at my side?

The word of God is, arguably, the most important thing I have. I must find, therefore, a good place to keep it. Ask where you should keep milk or medicine, and you'll get very specific and limited suggestions. But ask Moses, "Where shall I keep God's Law?" and he will answer emphatically, "Wherever you are!"

---

1   Dr. Seuss, *Green Eggs and Ham* (New York: Random House, 1988), 59–61.

Epilogue
God's Audience

It was not with our ancestors that the LORD made this covenant, but with us, with all of us who are alive here today.

Deuteronomy 5:3 NIV

We are coming full circle. We began our exploration of God's Law at Mount Sinai, the place where God first gave it to the children of Israel. And now, at the end, we return to Mount Sinai and the way that God gave that Law to those people.

Sinai was the austere and sacred mountain in the midst of the arid wilderness, the necessary stop between Egypt and the Promised Land. God appeared at the top of that mountain to give the people the Law. And gathered around the foot of that mountain was God's audience. I want us to see that audience.

There are at least several hundred thousand of them, according to census reports from a number of months later. And, in reality, the number may have been as many as three million. They are recently freed slaves who were presently living a kind of nomadic existence, journeying by stages through the desert. It is the nascent nation of Israel, gathered en masse around the base of Mount Sinai

The scene at Sinai is a picture of a great multitude. Yet in order for us to see the beauty of that multitude, we must rewind to see two earlier pictures of individuals. In contrast to the great crowd at Sinai, they are solitary figures talking with God.

Moses on the Mountain

The first picture comes from just a few months earlier, and the picture is taken at the exact same location: Mount Sinai. Before the nation of Israel met God there, you remember, Moses met God there. It was the burning bush episode, when the Lord appeared to Moses, and instructed him to go back to Egypt in order to free the Hebrew slaves.

The task, understandably, seemed impossible to Moses, and the assignment altogether undesirable. Accordingly, Moses tried to get out from under God's call. Yet the Lord kept insisting, and along the way God encouraged Moses with this promise: "Certainly I will be with you, and this shall be the sign to you that it is I who have sent you: when you have brought the people out of Egypt, you shall worship God at this mountain" (Exodus 3:12).

At that moment at the burning bush, you see, Moses was there alone with the Lord, and he was being given the impossible task of wresting the Hebrew slaves from Pharaoh's grip. And in the face of that daunting assignment, the Lord paints this happy prospect: the people gathered together in worship at that very mountain. So when you see the multitude there, assembled around the base of Mount Sinai, see it as a promise fulfilled.

Can you imagine how Moses might have looked down over that multitude? I imagine him remembering those weeks or months earlier when he stood there alone with God, and now he weeps tears of gratitude as he sees before him what the Lord has mightily accomplished since the burning bush.

Abraham Beneath the Sky

Meanwhile, the other scene of a solitary figure talking with God comes from several hundred years earlier and several hundred miles away. It happens back early in Genesis, when the Lord made a promise to Abraham one night.

Abraham had been faithful and obedient, and God had blessed him in many ways. Yet now he was an old man and still had none of the offspring that God had promised him. The Lord promised to have a special covenant relationship with Abraham's descendants, but Abraham *had* no descendants.

Then Genesis reports that the Lord "took [Abraham] outside and said, 'Now look toward the heavens, and count the stars, if you are able to count them.' And [the LORD] said to him, 'So shall your descendants be'" (Genesis 15:5).

Abraham was a solitary figure that night, but the Lord painted for him a compelling picture of a family that would rival the stars in the sky. And then, several hundred years later, assembled around Mount Sinai, God's promise was visibly true. There was the vast multitude of Abraham's descendants, and God was establishing his covenant with them.

God's covenant began like this: "I am the LORD thy God, which have brought thee out of the land of Egypt, out of the house of bondage. Thou shalt have no other gods before me." Then the Lord continued, "Thou shalt not make . . ." "Thou shalt not take . . ." "Thou shalt not . . ." "Thou shalt not . . ." "Thou shalt not . . ." On and on (Exodus 20 KJV).

It's a beautiful covenant. Just those segments, even without any of the following details, are beautiful. And I'd like to try to illustrate the beauty by sharing with you three, seemingly unrelated, personal experiences.

A Golfer, a Guitarist, and a Gideon

The first story comes from when I was perhaps ten years old. A PGA tournament was being hosted by a country club in the Cleveland area, where we lived at the time. One of the members of our church gave our family two passes to Sunday's round. My dad was unable to go, and so my mom and I went together.

We spent the day in the great entourage that was following Jack Nicklaus. Much of the time, we were in the middle or back of the crowd, using the cardboard periscopes that were provided to help us see. But at one particular hole, we had managed to find a place for ourselves right at the rope, directly behind where the players were going to tee off.

In addition to the players and caddies, a few PGA officials were walking around in that area within the ropes. And, of course, they have to stand somewhere while each player is hitting. And it happened that one of these officials stood right in front of me when Jack Nicklaus was walking up to hit his tee shot.

My mother, with the sort of chutzpah that only a mother can get away with, whispered to me—rather loudly—"Of all the places where he could have stood, why did he have to stand in front of a little boy who wanted to see Jack Nicklaus?!" Well, her whisper was loud enough that Mr. Nicklaus heard her! He turned around, and he motioned to the PGA official, asking him to move, which, of course, he did.

The second story comes from a number of years later, when I was twenty-five or so and a youth director. I took a group of my kids to a concert by a Christian band. It was an outdoor concert on a summer day at a big amusement park. Some folks in the crowd were sitting, but mostly we were a standing mob.

I expect that the audience was more visible to the band members than in a traditional indoor concert setting, with a lot of spotlights blinding them on stage. So there was a greater sense of connection with the performers. We weren't just looking at them; they were looking at us.

At one point, the lead singer made a remark aimed at the football fans in the audience, which prompted a number of us to hoot and wave our arms. Evidently he saw me, for he pointed to me and said, "There's a big fan!"

Finally, the third story comes from a few years later still, when I was pastoring two little churches in rural Virginia. One of the men in one of my congregations there was a member of the Gideons—an organization whose sole purpose is to distribute copies of the Bible. Well, this Gideon from my church invited me to come to a banquet that was being sponsored by the Gideons in the nearby town to honor all the pastors in the area.

After the dinner, before the main speaker for the evening, all of the Gideons who had brought their pastors with them were asked to stand and introduce them. So I was one of the several dozen pastors introduced to the crowd that night. And then, after those introductions were complete, the main speaker for the evening was introduced.

I had never met him before. I had never even heard of him. Yet when he came the podium, he immediately pointed at me and asked, "Were you a student at the University of Virginia about a dozen years ago?"

He was right—I had been. His prepared speech for that occasion, it turns out, was a series of testimonies of people whose lives were blessed by the ministry of the Gideons. And it so happened that one of the testimonies he was prepared to share that night was based on a letter I had written to the Gideons when I was in college. When he heard my church member introduce me by name, he realized it was the same as the name on the letter he had brought. And so, as soon as he stood up to speak, he singled me out in the crowd to confirm who I was.

The three stories have that common theme: the experience of being singled out in a crowd. It's a certain feeling of specialness. A heady experience that borders on discomfort because you don't feel quite worthy. Perhaps you've known the feeling somewhere along the way or enjoyed such a story of your own.

That is the scene I see at Sinai.

Special at Sinai

When we look at the scene at Mount Sinai, I am eager for us to sense something of that same heady experience for the children of Israel. Moreover, when you and I hear or read the Ten Commandments, I'd like for us have that same, special experience ourselves. It is the experience of being singled out in a crowd.

That was the specialness that I felt with the golfer at the tee, with the singer on stage, and with the Gideon at the podium. And that is the surprising specialness that is woven through the Ten Commandments.

This is a detail that you and I are apt to miss because of the limitations of our language. In the old King James Version of the English Bible, as we noted in an earlier chapter, we meet a distinction between *thou* and *ye*. Think of familiar and cherished passages like, "I will fear no evil: for *thou* art with me" (Psalm 23:4 KJV, emphasis added) and "Come unto me, all *ye* that labour and are heavy laden" (Matthew 11:28 KJV, emphasis added).

Thou and *ye* appear in the King James Version, but in our contemporary English translations, they would both just read "you." "I fear no evil, for *You* are with me" (NASB, emphasis added). "Come to me, all you" (NRSV). We do not as easily make the distinction in modern English between the singular *you* and the plural *you*.

Take that grammar, then, back to Mount Sinai, and look at what we see there, listen to what we hear there.

There is a great multitude of people gathered around the holy mountain—hundreds and hundreds of thousands of people. It is an NFL stadium times thirty! It is the night-sky-full of descendants that God had promised to Abraham, the new nation with which God was making God's covenant. And the Lord spoke to them and said, "*Thou.*" Not *ye*, but *thou*.

"*Thou* shalt have no other gods before Me." "*Thou* shalt not make . . ." "*Thou* shalt not take . . ." "*Thou* shalt not commit . . ." "*Thou* shalt not covet . . ." And so on. Go back to Mount Sinai and see that God speaks to a vast multitude, and God calls them *thou*.

The Sinai scene is profoundly beautiful because it is surprisingly intimate. There we observe our relentlessly personal God, who—even at this austere mountain, even at this undeniably national event—says, "I am the LORD *your* (singular, individual, personal) God, who brought *you* (singular, individual, personal) out of Egypt. You (singular, individual, personal) shall have no other gods before Me."

God is establishing a covenant with the nation of Israel, and God is doing it one person at a time. It is the specialness of being singled out in the midst of a crowd. And here it is none other than God who singles you out.

I saw a painting years ago that depicted a large congregation in church on a Sunday morning. The view was from the back row of a long cathedral, and as you looked down the aisle, you could see there was a considerable crowd, filling the pews. But there in the very back, there was a solitary worshiper in prayer. And in the painting, Jesus was seated next to him, arm around his shoulder, talking with him.

He meets with us together, to be sure, yet speaks to us one-on-one. It is singular, individual, personal. *Thou.*

When the Apostle Paul describes Jesus' second coming, he says, "The Lord Himself will descend from heaven with a shout" (1 Thessalonians 4:16). What do you suppose he will shout? The text doesn't say, but when I was a teenager, I heard someone speculate that when the Lord shouts, each of us will hear his or her own name.

I concede that the text doesn't say that, but I wouldn't be a bit surprised.

The man asked Jesus one day which of the commandments was the most important. And Jesus replied, "*Thou* [singular, individual, personal] shalt *love* the Lord *thy* [singular, individual, personal] God" (Matthew 22:37 KJV, emphasis added). For, you see, God loves you singularly, individually, and personally. And God wants your love to be the same.

Made in United States
North Haven, CT
16 June 2024

53667458R00088